CW01091067

NASEEB

NASEEB

by Naseem Shah

A

First published by Arena Books in 2024
www.arenabooks.co.uk

Naseeb
Naseem Shah

ISBN: 978-1-914390-29-6 Paperback
ISBN: 978-1-914390-35-7 Hardback
ISBN: 978-1-914390-30-2 Ebook

A Catalogue record for this book is available from the British Library.

Thema: DNBA; DNC; JBFH; 5PBC; JBFK3; JHBK; JBSL1; JKSN; NHTB; JBS; JBCC7; 1FKP; 5PBCG; 5PB-GB-AS; 3MPQ.

Cover design by Arena Books

To my children Amer, Ehmer, and Iram Shah.
My love for them kept me strong throughout my
rollercoaster life.

Family Tree

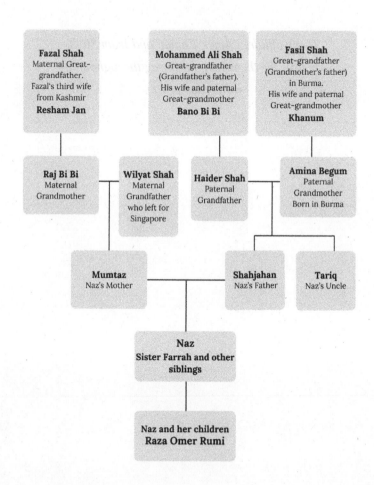

Fazal Shah
Maternal Great-grandfather.
Fazal's third wife from Kashmir
Resham Jan

Mohammed Ali Shah
Great-grandfather (Grandfather's father).
His wife and paternal Great-grandmother
Bano Bi Bi

Fasil Shah
Great-grandfather (Grandmother's father) in Burma.
His wife and paternal Great-grandmother
Khanum

Raj Bi Bi
Maternal Grandmother

Wilyat Shah
Maternal Grandfather who left for Singapore

Haider Shah
Paternal Grandfather

Amina Begum
Paternal Grandmother Born in Burma

Mumtaz
Naz's Mother

Shahjahan
Naz's Father

Tariq
Naz's Uncle

Naz
Sister Farrah and other siblings

Naz and her children
Raza Omer Rumi

Contents

Contents

I would like to say a very big thank you to my friend Marie McNay without whose careful and rigorous editing it would not have been possible to write this book.

Introduction

A s Naz was planting flowers and vegetables in her garden in the spring, she was carefully labelling them and wondering who would be living in this home in the future. She had lovingly renovated her home and decorated it with different shades of green. She had made herself a very comfortable place to live in the last few years, keeping in mind the future difficulties related to her health. The labels were for whoever was going to live in the house in the future so that they could enjoy the beauty of the garden and know what plants were where.

As her cancer was progressing to the advanced stage, Naz felt that she wanted to record her history, especially as her generation, who came to Britain in the late 1950s and early 1960s, was now dying. She wanted to record the experiences of her background, her marriage and immigration to Britain, and to reflect on her evolving identity and her destiny - both as it was assumed at birth and the destiny that she ultimately arrived at. She had been born in India into a very traditional rural Pir family, which had a strong influence on her outlook and values, but she also grew up under the influence of the retreating British Raj and was strongly influenced by the colonial background of the period.

Even today, more than 75 years after the British Raj ended, Naz felt that there was still a need to explain why people from the former colonies came to Britain. What were the circumstances in which they lived? And what were the gains and losses in making new homes in Britain? The climate, the culture, and the conditions were, and still are, totally different from the subcontinent of India. The only common thread at the time was a type of British culture, since the Raj had dominated the subcontinent for almost two hundred years.

When Naz was growing up, she heard many stories sitting on the laps of her grandparents, uncles and aunties. These were stories about how the family and their ancestors lived and what relationships they had with each other, and their relationship with the colonial masters who believed in their own superiority. There were stories both of personal bravery and defeat; stories of standing up to their masters and maintaining dignity and traditions, while at other times giving up because the local circumstances were such that they had to subdue their individual culture and traditions. This relationship of being subjugated continued into the 1950s and 1960s, when most of the migration from Pakistan to Britain took place.

During this period, workers came to Britain

because the ex-colonial masters in the form of the British government were asking people from the former colonies to come to help rebuild the economy and the health of Britain after the second world war. People were invited to work in the NHS as doctors, nurses or as labourers, working in the factories in the north of Britain. At this time, it has been suggested that the former colonies lost out through having so many skilled and unskilled men in their 20s and 30s leaving to work in the 'mother country.' Britain also exploited India during this time by importing raw materials from India without tariffs, and then adding value through the manufacture of goods and selling these goods back to India at higher prices.

Immigrants from India and Pakistan were employed mainly as labourers, working in factories or hospitals as porters and other unskilled and low-paid jobs, though some later got jobs driving buses which was considered more skilful. It did not matter whether these people were qualified professionals, like teachers, or not, because their qualifications and skills were not recognised. People who went to Britain specifically to undertake higher education were from a different class to the vast majority of economic immigrants and were equally remote. Initially, when men and women came to Britain to work, they were totally unaware of what kind of issues they would have to face, whether it was housing, jobs, or (especially) racism. The women who came over faced even greater challenges. They were mostly dependent on their husbands at that time and endured a whole host of problems, especially when it came to the language and dealing with officials and institutions.

All Asians may look the same to some white British people and similarly, to some Asians, all white Europeans look the same. However, the Asians from the subcontinent were not a homogeneous group. It is said that along every ten miles of that country, the food, the dialect and the subculture of people changes. But, as an immigrant, one's identity becomes blurred. Asian people in their own country are recognised by their clan or tribe, or by their home villages and towns. By contrast, in Britain, their identities became linked to their jobs, like bus driver, shopkeeper, waiter, or hospital porter. Naz remembered once that when she was in a swimming pool, a lady approached her and complained about the newspapers not being delivered, thinking Naz must be from the local corner shop that sold newspapers. Another time, Naz was in a pub in Gateshead with a Palestinian friend who looked entirely different to Naz except for their similar skin colour. A man came over and asked whether they were sisters. Naz asked him whether all the white men in the pub were his brothers. Naz thought that if this was a pickup line, it was terrible! And if he really thought they were sisters, it was even worse.

Most immigrants intended to return after they had made enough money, but for most, this did not happen. This was mostly due to low wages, and the longer they stayed and had families and children starting school, the more difficult it became to return.

For various reasons, parents' experiences are different to their children's and to subsequent generations.

The experiences of the immigrants who came over in the 1970s and after were different from those of the 1950s and 1960s, who were largely uneducated and came mainly as labourers. The generations who arrived in the 1970s increasingly came as skilled and professional workers. These later generations benefitted from the Race Relations Acts of 1965 and 1968. The 1965 Act "prohibited racial discrimination in public places," and made the "promotion of hatred on the grounds of colour, race, or ethnic or national origin, an offence."

This meant that it was illegal, for example, to display a sign saying "No blacks, no dogs, and no Irish," outside shops, factories and houses. This meant that, at least in theory, shopping, jobs, and renting rooms or houses, could not be refused to immigrants. The subsequent 1968 Act prohibited British people from being overtly racist. Although this didn't solve all problems overnight, it did help the later generations to do relatively well, financially, educationally and socially. It would be fair to say that many of their forerunners and parents played a major part in this success.

It was during the earlier period that Naz came to Britain and lived her adult life. Her story is both a product of this history and the result of different immigration processes and circumstances, but it is also the story of an individual woman. Facing the end of her life, she reflects on the person she was and has become – someone who was born in the middle of one century on one continent and who will die in the earlier part of the following century on another continent. She evolved from this beginning through many challenges to arrive at an identity, and a destiny, that she could not have foreseen.

Chapter 1

Colonial Past

Naseeb was born in Northern India in 1945 into a very traditional rural Pir family. A year or two later, the family moved to Pakistan and luckily were not caught up in the severe consequences of the Partition. As the oldest child of very young parents, she was brought up amongst grandparents, great grandparents, and lots of uncles and aunties. These uncles and aunties were the younger siblings of both her mother and father. Some were her age, and some were a bit older. This extended family lived together and moved together as one family for many years. They were influenced throughout their lives by the colonial background of the period and at the same time, were strongly influenced by the family, culture and *biradari* (the brotherhood or fraternity/community).

Naseeb's great grandfather, Fasil Shah, was in the 9th Lancers regiment stationed in Delhi. Bahadur Shah Zafar II was the last Mughal King and Emperor of Hindustan, and his home was also in Delhi which had been the traditional homeplace and centre of the Mughal empire for centuries. For this reason, the British decided that it was an important strategic location and should come under their control. In 1857, after capturing the Red Fort in Delhi under the command of British general William Hodson, Bahadur Shah Zafar was arrested. A mock court case followed and the emperor was found guilty of plotting an uprising and revolt against the British. Following the kangaroo court's decision, the emperor's sons and grandsons were shot and then beheaded. Soon after, the emperor and the rest of his family were put upon a ship and exiled to Rangoon. The family were escorted by the 9th Lancers regiment who also took their families, including Fasil Shah's family. The King died in 1862 and Fasil Shah's family stayed in Burma (now Myanmar) for several years until a ship to Multan became available. Naseeb's paternal grandmother, Amina, was born on the ship, coming back from Rangoon (now Yangon) to India. Her parents were from Multan (then in British India, now South Pakistan), which was why they went there on their return from Burma. Later in life, Naseeb's great grandmother, Khanum, would tell stories to Amina of Burma and of the inhuman and undignified treatment that the emperor king endured there in his last years.

Naseeb's ancestors had travelled from Iraq into Iran and settled in Multan. The main head of the clan, Sheikh Bahauddin Zakariya, remained there, but the rest of the clan travelled and settled all over the sub-continent. Later, some of her clan moved to a village called Keruli (because of marriage connections), an area with very high mountains and a rugged terrain. Legend has it that when some members of the family went to live in the mountains, there was no water for them to wash and pray. So, one of them fetched a small amount of water from somewhere, washed his mouth and gargled, and since that time, there have been waterfalls in the village. Therefore, the village was called Keruli, meaning 'gargle.'

The ancestors were mainly Sufis and Darwish and were therefore called Pirs (head of spiritual leaders). It was a common belief that they performed miracles as well as spiritual healings. They were peace-loving people, well versed in the Quran and its meaning, and other religious books as well as poetry. They were close to Moguls, because Royals tended to seek guidance and spiritual healings from the Pirs. Sheikh Bahauddin Zakariya, whose shrine is in Multan, was one of the Pir elders. He was well known for his promotion of business, vocational, and recreational activities, including trade and youth clubs. As he was very wealthy at that time, he loaned money without interest to people all over the subcontinent so that they could be traders and improve their business. They had (and still have) millions of followers and believers, including people from other religions, not just on the subcontinent but beyond. The Pirs also have grand shrines throughout the subcontinent where thousands of people visit every day and pray for their spiritual and earthly welfare.

The very high mountains surrounding the village of Keruli were covered with wild olive trees. Most people were from the same clan and it was a tightknit community. The village was divided into two areas, one at the lower end of the village and the other higher up on the mountain. At the bottom of the village, there were massive waterfalls and fruit gardens spread out for miles. The main and very special fruit were loquat and grapes. There were wild peacocks and deer in the gardens. The women regularly got together and sometimes took their children to the waterfalls where they would wash and dry their clothes as well as bathe themselves and their children. Lots of gossip and intermingling went on amongst the women in the gardens. It was mostly a day out for the women and children. Men stayed away from that area out of respect for the women. There were very strict customs and practices because it was mostly one clan spread out in the entire village. All women and girls were considered everyone's sisters, daughters or mothers as a mark of respect. For example, if a male member of the village was passing in front of someone's front door, he would make them aware by coughing in case there was a female member inside without her head covered or simply just to alert them to his presence. At the bottom of the village on the other side, there was a very large and old Banyan tree which young men would sit under to gossip and talk. The older men would hold *girga* or *punciat* (well-known practices on the subcontinent which still exist in some areas) to make decisions. The decisions made by the *girga* or *punciat* were accepted and acted on.

As there was no running water and electricity in the village, the water and kerosene oil for the light were supplied on mules. The fruits, flowers and vegetables were sold and delivered by the people who ran the gardens. People had their own chickens and eggs in the house. For other meat, someone in the village would halal their sheep, or cow and announce this in the village and then it would be shared with others for money. The livelihoods of men were either farming goats and cattle or they left to work in big cities.

The men and women from the village were mostly strong and hardy, and this was one of the reasons a lot of men were recruited to the British army, especially in the Second World War. Some men were made prisoners of war in Germany and later released and came back to the village. The village people, mostly women, had no idea about the war. They didn't know why it was happening or where it was, and even the men who were there knew very little about it. A very popular story that sons told their mothers was that they were going to fight Hitler. One mother was very upset and crying constantly, worrying about her son Muhammed Khan who was very stubborn and never gave up. She had heard that Hitler was a very nasty piece of work and wondered how this fight was going to end. The poor woman imagined a one-to-one fight with Hitler. The concept of a world war did not exist in their minds.

A marriage was arranged for Naseeb's paternal grandmother, Amina, with Hadier Shah, Naseeb's grandfather. It took place in Keruli. Hadier Shah was from the same clan and they were related by ancestry. He was a soldier in the British Army, but the headquarters were in Delhi where the family lived. When he was posted to the Northwest frontier, the family went to Keruli. He was in the artillery regiment fighting on the borders of Afghanistan. Hadier Shah used to talk about the hardship and the cruel training that took place in Afghanistan. He also told stories about one of the British Regiments who wore frocks with bare legs and long socks. Later, Naseeb realised it must be a Scottish regiment who were wearing kilts. Her grandfather was given a sword for bravery, which he was very proud of and looked after until the end of his life. He left the army when he started to grow a beard, customary in the family at a certain age. He always told the story of why he left the army with a lot of pride, saying that the Colonel said, "'either you wear a beard or a uniform,' and I said 'I will wear a beard,'" and so he was dismissed.

Hadier Shah's brother, Wilayet Shah, was also in Delhi, managing a British club. The name Wilayet Shah translated meant 'Britania Shah.' He was very good looking, tall and handsome with very light skin, which is considered good looking in the Indian Sub-Continent. Due to his light skin, he could pass as Anglo Indian and therefore considered suitable to manage a British club. He enjoyed his job and all the perks it offered. As an Anglo-Indian employee, he was entitled to take home whisky, gin, and other drinks for his weekly allowance. As a Muslim, he never drank alcohol, but the story is told that he used to give it to the neighbours. It is thought that had he refused to take his allowance, the club would find out he was Indian (not Anglo Indian) and he would probably get the sack.

Some years earlier, the two brothers, Walayat Shah and Haider Shah, were living together in one house with their respective wives. Haider Shah's wife Amina had a healthy son and, being the first son, lots of celebrations took place. The parents were barely eighteen. They named their son Shahjahan after the Mogul King. The expectations were that in time, the boy would grow up and would be able to earn and contribute income to the extended family. Six months after Shahjahan's birth, Wilayet Shah's wife Raj Bi Bi gave birth to a beautiful daughter. Wilayet Shah wrapped his baby in a blanket and brought her out in the courtyard to show off to his brother and the rest of the family. His brother Haider Shah took the baby in his arms and with lots of love and excitement said to his wife and the baby's father, "Look, Shahjahan's future wife has been born and her name is Mumtaz." No one questioned this statement, and the babies became engaged, involving extra celebrations. Sweets called ludos, always eaten and shared as a treat at celebrations, were distributed in the neighbourhood for the double celebrations. At that point, the mother was recovering from childbirth in a room with some of her relatives and knew nothing of the arrangement, but the news was shared afterwards with the biradari.

The children grew up together as brother and sister, unaware of the marriage arrangement made by the parents. During this time both parents had a lot more children and carried on living together until Haider Shah had to go to the Northwest frontier and Afghanistan with the British Army, and his wife and children went to the village Keruli where his parents and his extended family still lived. Uncertain about when he would come back, he thought it best that his family lived in the village. His oldest son, Shahjahan, was sent to the military college boarding school in Punjab run by the British. Spread on 172 acres of lush land in Jhelum, it was founded by the Prince of Wales, Prince Edward VIII and named King

George Royal Indian Military School (KGRIMS).

Wilayet Shah was running the club and earning good money in Delhi, living a good life, along with his family. The children were going to good schools and had lots of animals, goats, cows, buffalos and dogs, which they loved. The club members and the staff used to go to Shimla British Hill station in the summer and back to Delhi in the winter. Wilayet Shah and his family accompanied the club staff to Shimla for a few years until Wilayet Shah was sent to Singapore by the British club owners, as they planned to set up a new club there. He was not allowed to take his family, but also his children were too young to travel such a long way. He left behind his twenty-five-year-old wife and four children in Delhi. Travelling was difficult, so he never came back. He later married again in Singapore and started a life with another wife and had children. He couldn't have an illicit relationship because it was not allowed in the Muslim religion, but he was allowed to marry as he had not lived with his first wife for some time. He lived there until he died of old age.

After living in Delhi for a few years without Wilayet Shah, this family also decided to move back to the village of Keruli and be with the extended family. So, both Wilayet Shah's and Haider Shah's families were in the same village (Haider Shah had returned there from the Northwest Frontier when he was dismissed from the army). Throughout this time, Wilayet Shah kept sending money to his first wife and children as well as to his parents and anyone else in the village who did not have any other source of income because it was a tradition to support families.

Naseeb's maternal great grandmother Resham Jan came from Kashmir and her great grandfather, Fazal Shah, came from Keruli. He was a Pir like the rest of the biradari. The Collins English dictionary defines Pir as 'a term of respect for the head of a religious group, especially in Pakistan, various areas of the Middle East and Near East.' Fazal Shah was referred to as Pir Sahib and he mostly travelled to Kashmir from Punjab for business. He took pink Himalayan salt and a few other products from Punjab to sell in Kashmir. Similarly, he brought back products from Kashmir to Punjab, selling them there for profit. He travelled on horses with an entourage and on their way, they would stop overnight in some places for refreshments with people who followed him. They felt honoured to be hosting Fazal Shah and his associates.

Pir Sahib had married three times and the wives all came from Kashmir. The first wife had one daughter, and she died in Punjab. The second wife died in childbirth and the surviving baby daughter was brought up by the extended family in the village. Fazal Shah loved his second wife very much, and it took him a very long time to recover from her death. When he was on one of his business trips, he stayed at the home of one of his followers in Kashmir. His host felt very privileged that Pir Sahib was staying at their home and could not do enough to please him. Taking this opportunity, Pir Sahib asked for their daughter's hand in marriage and the host happily accepted. A simple ceremony took place and Fazal Shah married his third wife, Naseeb's maternal great grandmother.

The bride was very young and had never been away

from home or from her immediate family. She was put on horseback behind her husband's horse and she cried all the way to the village in Punjab, which was several days' journey. Everything was new for her – food, language, clothes, weather – even the terrain was very unfamiliar. She felt very lonely and was often frightened. The village of Keruli was miles away from any other community or civilization, or a proper road for that matter, and people could only travel on horses or camels. It was surrounded by very high mountains, which were known as a habitat for wild animals. Often the livestock was stolen by wolves. The bride was made welcome by the extended family and after a few years, she settled with her children and her husband.

Naseeb's father, Shahjahan, got an excellent education and training at the King George Royal Military college. He spoke perfect English because the college wanted the students to become 'British.' He was quite a character, and at school, he was always encouraged to be outspoken and give his opinion, so he would forget that young people were not allowed to interfere or speak out in front of the elders. One time, the elders were arranging someone's marriage and holding court under the banyan tree. There were some youngsters there, strictly for observation, and Shahjahan was there too. The elders were trying to work out the age of the prospective bride, but there was some uncertainty. When Shahjahan saw that the elders were struggling, he said to the elders, "Just ask the young lady how long she has been having her periods." Everyone went into shock for a moment, but when the elders fully realised what Shahjahan had said, his grandfather stood up to beat him with his stick. Shahjahan was a sportsman and sensed danger, so he made a run for it. Shahjahan's father and uncles started running after him, followed by the rest of the clan, chasing him all over the village. At that time and even now, women's periods are not mentioned openly, particularly in public. This story was whispered in the village for years to come.

Shahjahan had very good prospects in the future. During the holidays, he came back to the village where he was invited by the biradari for meals and events in their homes. At college, he had been taught to use cutlery, and he had almost forgotten how to eat with his hands, so he used to take his cutlery with him, stuck in his front jacket pocket like one would have stuck a pen. Naseeb's mother, Mumtaz, had been educated in Delhi, but this was discontinued when the family moved to the village when she was about twelve years old. Therefore, her family was not considered to be at an equal level to that of Shahjahan's family.

Around this time, there were reports from Singapore (which turned out to be true) that (Wilayet Shah) Naseeb's maternal grandfather had married again to a local woman and had a family in Singapore. As he could no longer afford to send as much money back to his family in the village, the funds were drying up for that family and others. When this happened, members of the biradari in the village distanced themselves from Mumtaz's family. Shahjahan's family had also distanced themselves, so it was a very hard time for Mumtaz's family.

Rumours came via the biradari that ShahJahan's parents

were not sure about the engagement with Mumtaz which had taken place years ago. A message was sent to Shahjahan's family to confirm or deny the rumours. Unfortunately, the rumours were confirmed. Shahjahan's family said that now that their son was well educated and had very bright prospects, the old arrangements were not possible.

Mumtaz's mother, Raj Bi Bi, was beside herself with stress and worry as this would bring disgrace to the family. And, because her daughter was of marriageable age, the breaking of the contract would make her unmarriageable. She was crying and wailing to everyone and did not know where to turn. Mumtaz's siblings — two sons and another daughter — were too young to understand anything. Raj Bi Bi thought she would never be able to see this marriage taking place, even though she had saved a dowry for her daughter and her future son-in-law when she had had the money. The blunt refusal from Shahjahan's family was a hard blow. Her husband was far away in Singapore with his new family and it was not possible to get in touch with him, but in any case, he was gradually taking less and less interest in his first family.

When Mumtaz saw her mother feeling so helpless, she consoled her and told her to leave it to her. The next morning, she got ready after breakfast and told her mother that she was going to see Shahjahn's parents. Her mother told her not to take such a drastic step, stating this was not the 'done thing' in the village and may cause an even bigger problem. It was unheard of for a young woman to discuss her marriage, even with her own elders. These things are usually discussed and decided amongst the male elders, not even the women, let alone young girls, especially the girl it concerned. Even now, some decades later, when girls are taken back from Britain to the Indian subcontinent for the purpose of marriage, the girls find it hard to stand up to the elders or the extended family. Mumtaz was determined to do something as she could not bear her mother crying all the time and feeling totally helpless. She was very independent and put on her outdoor clothing, her chador, and walked to Shahjahn's parents' house.

After asking them about their welfare, she told Shahjahan's parents the reason she was there. She asked whether the rumour about breaking the engagement was true. They did not deny it and further said that now that their son was educated, they wished to find an educated wife for him. Mumtaz reminded them about the arrangements between her parents and themselves, which had taken place fifteen years earlier. She told them that now that her father was miles away and there was very little chance of him coming back to her mother and herself, they were on their own without any adult male in the family. She emphasised that it would not look good with the biradari and that they were letting the family down. She said that they had to honour their arrangement; that it was traditional and a contract of honour. She further emphasised the fact that the entire village was aware of this arrangement and therefore it would not be possible for them to break it.

After spending some hours with them, Mumtaz walked back home through the narrow pebble streets. All the pent-up anger and anxiety were released, and she cried her heart out. She was crying because she had to do this where, in other circumstances, it would have been her father or elder brother. She badly missed not having her father there.

The day after she reassured her mother, Mumtaz sent a message to the military college where Shahjahan, whom she regarded as her fiancée, was studying, which asked him to come home as soon as possible. When he came back to the village, he went to visit Mumtaz and her family. He was told about the present situation and the consequences of breaking off the agreement. Shahjahan was quite unaware of this arrangement and confused about the circumstances, but willing to listen to Mumtaz and her mother. He was persuaded by them to go and talk to his parents and set a date for the wedding. The date was set for immediately after Shahjahan's graduation.

The wedding was a village affair. Everyone participated and there was lots of singing, dancing, food and sweets. It was a very happy occasion, but people talked about the missing father, Walayat Shah. Some people cried openly for him, because he was a kind man who was brought up in this village and who had financially supported some people. Walayat Shah's father, mother, siblings, his children and his friends were very sad because he was well thought of and he was missing the important occasion of his first daughter's marriage.

Mumtaz moved into the home of her in-laws, according to tradition. She was the dominant spouse and for the next sixty years, told Shahjahn what to do. He followed her orders because she was much sharper and cleverer than him and, generally, he was a thorough gentleman and trusting fellow.

The marriage worked out well and proved to be a happy union for both.

Chapter 2

Early Childhood

After the wedding, as Shahjahan had graduated, he was employed in the Royal Air Force and transferred to the city of Bangalore in South India for a short training. Mumtaz accompanied her husband, despite a lot of opposition from his parents. They were told they were too young to be living in a strange city on their own and Mumtaz would be alone while Shahjahan was working. It was not thought safe for a young woman to be living on her own while her husband was training. They also thought a young girl should not be taking this journey alone (because men and women travelled in separate compartments). There was a lot of discussion for and against the idea. Mumtaz herself was very concerned in case she was left behind to do all the work in the house. Finally, some elders, including Mumtaz and Shahjahn's grandparents, got involved in making the decision and Mumtaz was allowed to go with her husband.

The camels were booked in advance at dawn for the

journey from the village to the nearest railway station, to ensure the booking and that they did not miss the train connection. The camels wore bells round their necks which would tinkle and was a sign that someone from the village was travelling. This was exciting for the villagers and is a very pleasant memory now.

The railway station was several miles away in a very sleepy town with only one train per day going to a big junction where people could take another train to Bangalore. The camels always leave the village just before dawn. It was a slow journey because camels take their time walking leisurely up and down the mountains, nibbling every bush and tree they come across. The custom was that male passengers and the camel driver walk beside the camels whilst the luggage, women, children, disabled and old ride on the camels. When the Pir family especially travelled on the camels, people in the nearby villages would often stand on the route with some refreshments like Lassi butter milk and some food or homemade sweets.

Mumtaz was excited and very happy, as it would be the first time she would be alone with her husband. She no longer had to obey orders and work from morning till night at her in-laws' home. As the eldest daughter-in-law, she had had to assume all the household responsibilities. This included cleaning and cooking for her father-in-law Haider Shah and mother-in-law Amina, plus their six children, aged from sixteen to one year. Mumtaz packed all her beautiful dowry clothes, shoes, and jewellery, which were loaded on the camels the next morning.

After the arduous camel journey and exhausting long train journey, they arrived in Bangalore. Mumtaz enjoyed the new city. Everything was different – the climate was tropical in comparison to the village, which had four very distinct seasons. She loved the different language, and the fruits and flowers were totally different from what they had in the village. What she remembered most were lots of coconuts and monkeys in the gardens. She embraced the differences and didn't find a problem settling in. Her formative years as a young adult were in this big city, Dehli.

But just as they had got used to their newfound freedom, Shahjahan was transferred to Jalandhar, Punjab in North India and Mumtaz also became pregnant at that time. The train journey from Bangalore to Jalandhar was very long, taking a few days and nights. The entire regiment was moving to Punjab, and the men were in separate compartments from the women. At every station, as the train stopped, Shahjahan would come to the window and ask Mumtaz if she wanted to eat anything. All she wanted was to use the toilet, but the toilet was dirty and she was hesitant to ask Shahjahan to request that the toilets be cleaned. Eventually she did ask him and at one station, when the train stopped for longer, he got someone to clean the toilets. Mumtaz became popular with the women in her compartment for getting things done.

They had hardly arrived in their new home in Jalandhar when the news of Mumtaz being pregnant, and the fact that they had moved to Punjab, reached the village. The next thing they knew, Shahjahan's parents, Haider Shah and Amina, and the other six children arrived in Jalandhar to live with them, as it was a tradition for the husband's extended family to live in their son's house. Another very good reason from their point of view was that Mumtaz was giving birth and would require advice and help from the family. A few weeks later, Mumtaz's mother, Raj Bi Bi, and her siblings (Naseeb's aunties and uncles), also arrived to help the expectant mother.

Mumtaz gave birth to a girl at home with the help of a midwife and her family. Everyone was happy except Amina, the paternal grandmother. She loved Shahjahan very much and had high aspirations for him, so she was disappointed. The baby was not a boy, and the traditional hope was that the first-born child would be a son who would contribute financially. Also, the baby was more brown than fair, and very light skin was considered more beautiful. The only other person in that family who was the same darker colour as the baby was Amina herself. So these feelings reflected traditional norms but were enhanced by Amina's aspirations for Shahjahan.

There were some celebrations but not as many ludos were distributed in the neighbourhood. After some deliberations, the family decided that the name would be Naseeb, which means fate or karma. In the subcontinent, unfortunately, the birth of a daughter as the first child is not seen as an auspicious occasion. And this was even more so seventy years ago when Naseeb was born. Even if the parents were happy, the grandparents would not want a girl, so Mumtaz and Shahjhan had very little say in the name. Naseeb is always a female name and males are rarely given this name. Parents are filled with apprehension when a girl is born before a boy, always afraid of her *naseeb* (translated as 'destiny') because her happiness is thought to depend on her future husband and his family.

Naseeb (also spelt Nesib, Nasib or Nasip) is an Arabic term used in many countries and languages. The literal translation is 'share,' but it has come to be understood as 'one's share in life,' and therefore a person's 'destiny.' The name is used frequently in the sub-continent for some traditions, but not with boys. For example, when older people meet or say goodbye to a younger person, it is customary to offer them good wishes. However, if it is a girl or unmarried woman, they will usually wish her a good naseeb. The underlying meaning is that the person is wished a good husband and to have a good future. Naseeb is not used with boys who are wished a long life and happiness. The word differentiates girls from boys and is an indication that they could have a good or bad future, depending on who they marry.

In Naseeb's case, everyone was expecting the first born to be a boy, so it was not a good naseeb or good omen. The expectation is that a boy will grow up and contribute to the family income, an aid to his father. Naseeb's parents were very young and as girls were, and still are, considered of marriageable age soon after puberty, this would mean more pressure on the family. As her father, Shahjahan would have the cost of her marriage and dowry when he was still young. He was also the oldest in his family and would have responsibility for his parents and siblings. So, there were two reasons for giving Naseeb this name. Firstly, it was the parents' fate at such a young age that the first born was a girl – it was thought to be bad luck. Secondly, as a girl, it was thought that her fate could be good, i.e., good karma, but it might not be. The hope was that it would be the former, but either way, it did not sound like they were very optimistic. No one could predict what kind of husband Naseeb would have, so it was thought that it would have been better if the baby had not been a girl.

However, Naseeb had lots of love and affection and attention from the extended family. The house was full of grandparents as well as young uncles and aunties, everyone competing to carry the baby or play with her. Often, they had bets and whoever won the bet could hold the baby. Mumtaz herself had very little chance to spend time with the baby, or change or bath her, but she was quite happy to have a good night's sleep and a rest.

Quite often, the male members of the family would take Naseeb away from the house, so the female members could not follow them. Or the women would take her to the roof of the house and lock the door to keep everyone out. Naseeb seemed to enjoy all the attention and thrived. Some ideas of bonding in Western culture, for example, attachment theory, where a child is thought to form the main bond with one or two primary caregivers, are very different from cultures. In some countries, several close relatives living in one household all take part in the caring and give lots of love, which does change the intensity of the relationships. Sometimes, when children grow up in an extended family, there may be several female and male adult relatives who are the same age as the child's mother or father. The child will use another word for mother and father for adults in the household who are not the biological parents. The concept of the nuclear family with one mother and one father being in the household is more a Western notion, coined in the early twentieth century when family patterns were changing. In many other cultures, it is one woman who gives birth, but there could be several women (and men) in the house, looking after children. If there are two women who are of child-bearing age, it is not unknown for one woman to breast feed another woman's child.

Naseeb was born as the Second World War ended and the British were leaving India. The partition of India was about to happen and there was a lot going on in the sub-Continent. Naseeb was only a few weeks old when there was a victory parade, which everyone wanted to go and see. Very small children were not allowed to go, but everyone in the house went to see the parade and join the celebrations, including Naseeb. She was smuggled in a large piece of cloth, a chador, and listened to the band but stayed very quiet, which helped the grown-ups' conspiracy.

The family continued to compete to show who loved her the most, and all bought presents for her. Whatever little money they had was spent on Naseeb. They bought her silver bangles with bells on and had her ears pierced with little gold earrings. They bought her a gold chain and silver ankle chains, which also had bells. One day, someone in the family bought her a very fancy jewellery box to put all her jewellery in. A few days later, they had a robbery. In the middle of the night, a man came over the courtyard wall and saw the jewellery box, which was left in the yard. He didn't know what was in the box, but he must have thought there would be expensive jewellery in it. He picked up the box and put it on the wall. As he was climbing up the wall to get out, Naseeb's grandmother, Amina, woke up and saw him. Amina was tall and a very sturdy woman and she pushed the robber over the other side of the wall and picked up the jewellery box. Next morning, she told everyone, and they were surprised that she hadn't bothered to wake anyone or even shout to raise the alarm. She was that sort of woman, bold and straight talking and well known for her bravery and courage.

Shahjahan made lots of friends in the city of Jalandhar and became quite popular. He was very good at playing hockey and was in a very good team in the RAF. He visited other cities in India to play hockey with other teams.

These were changing times. The British Raj was ending, as was the Second World War. The troops were returning to their regiments or travelling back home. In 1945, the Labour party came to power in Britain and it seemed that India's independence was imminent. There was also news that negotiations were going on about Muslims having their own country, that a separate country was being created for them, a partition. Mahatma Gandhi and the Congress leadership were against this partition of India. The All India Radio broadcaster was giving news about discussions, heated arguments, riots, massacres and lootings that were taking place. Strong tensions were building.

It is reported that the border between the two new states of Pakistan and India was hurriedly drawn up by a British lawyer, Cyril Radcliffe, who had little knowledge of Indian conditions and with the use of out-of-date maps and census materials. Communities, farms and families were crudely cut in two.

The creation of the new countries brought an unprecedented movement of people across the new border, and horrific consequences of disruption, civil disorder and violence. No one knew exactly where they were going or what future lay ahead. People who had lived in the same communities for decades became suspicious and sometimes hostile to their neighbours. Others put their lives at risk and protected their neighbours and provided refuge for them. Most people left in such a hurry that they did not have time to pack their essentials. There are stories that some people left their gold and other valuables with their neighbours for safe keeping, thinking they would return after a few years to collect them. Others buried their valuables in the houses they were leaving, hoping to dig them out when the situation calmed down. In the mass movement of people, not all Muslims moved to Pakistan and similarly not all Hindus and Sikhs moved to India. It is estimated that around two million people were killed during the partition.

Earlier in this period, Naseeb's family could see that things were getting difficult in India, but fortunately Shahjahan was posted to Peshawar, a city in the Northwest Frontier of Pakistan. The extended family split up for practical reasons and Shahjahan, Mumtaz, Naseeb, grandmother Raj Bi Bi, one young auntie Layla and young Uncle Tariq all went to Peshawar. The other elders went back to the village, Keruli, in Pakistan, where they still had lots of extended family living.

It was only a temporary move until the younger members of the family, who were becoming young adults, could find employment and accommodation and move to Rawalpindi in Pakistan.

In Peshawar, Shahjahan was offered very nice accommodation through the RAF. Everyone was happy to be safe, and happy that they had avoided any violence or other difficulties which other people were experiencing. Grandmother Raj Bi Bi and auntie Layla looked after the kitchen and other household jobs while Mumtaz, being a lady of leisure who enjoyed a social life more than work, and also pregnant again, rested and managed everyone. At that time, she got rid of her chador. When the news reached the elders in the village, they objected to this 'chadorless' Mumtaz very strongly, particularly Hadier Shah and Amina. Their fear was that, as this was the first time Mumtaz had been far away from them for a long time, she would get out of control. Elders always wanted to make sure that the young ones kept the traditions. However, Mumtaz was not going to give up her control easily. She sent a message back that she was pregnant again and that the doctors had advised her strongly that she must not wear a chador and that she needed plenty of fresh air. This was not strictly true. Mumtaz was expecting a baby, but the fresh air part was untrue. Hearing both reasons, the elders gave up at this stage and did not pursue the matter any further.

Shahjahan spent a lot of time playing hockey and enjoyed being in the RAF at this time. As Mumtaz was without the chador, Shahjahan was also able to resist norms and get a dog, an Alsatian. Shahjahan loved the dog, as did Naseeb. In those days, people used to have English names for their dogs and spoke English to them, so the dog was called Jack. In Pakistan, there was no tinned food for dogs, so Shahjahan used to buy bones and meat from the butchers to cook for Jack every day. Everyone knew that Shahjahan was very fond of Jack. One day, Raj Bi Bi went to the market, still wearing her white shuttlecock burqa, and Jack followed her. She only noticed him when she was carrying fruit and vegetable bags in both hands. She was very concerned about Jack's safety, but the only words she knew in English were 'come on.' When she shouted this, Jack started jumping on her and pushing her. The only other words she knew in English, which she must have learned when she was living in British Delhi, were 'fuck off.' When Jack was jumping on her and pushing her, she shouted this. So, one minute, Jack was told to come on and the next to fuck off. People in the market were well entertained.

Grandfather Hadier Shah heard about the dog and wrote a long letter to Shahjahan very strongly objecting to it being in the house. He thought dogs were dirty animals and asked how Shahjahan was going to say his payers. Letting his wife go out without a chador was one thing, but keeping a dog was another. He told Shahjahan to get rid of the dog immediately. Unlike Mumtaz, Shahjahan didn't make excuses for keeping the dog in the house but didn't oblige either. Hadier Shah further wrote that this behaviour was all due to Shahjahan's education and training in the British Military college. At that point, it seemed like he was regretting sending his son to get a British education, though all his life he had been very proud of that. The falling away of traditional norms that can occur when children have had an education was difficult for the older generation. The elders in the village were also concerned that Shahjahan and Mumtaz had become a modern couple, and that they may neglect the extended family, the biradari, and the family traditions.

Mumtaz gave birth to a second girl in Lady Reading Hospital, a Combined Military Hospital (CMH) that was established in 1927. The hospital was named after the highest ranked British Jewish officer's wife. The hospital still exists and is fully functioning. The baby was fair like her parents and very beautiful and healthy. She was named Farah, which means lovely, pleasant and good looking. She was more like her maternal grandmother Raj Bi Bi, whose mother came from Kashmir.

Naseeb was a toddler by then. She loved playing with the dog and trying to teach him new tricks, like climbing on the chair. And she loved turning on the radio and listening to the music and dancing on request. While Farah was just getting fed and sleeping as a very small baby, Naseeb talked a lot to make sure that she stayed the centre of attention a bit longer.

Chapter 3

Childhood

A fter a few years in Peshawar, Shahjahan was posted to Risalpur, a cantonment city northeast of Peshawar. Risalpur had been a former aerodrome and airfield of the Royal Flying Corps, which was used by British India from 1910 onward and during the First and Second World Wars. The city is on the Northwest Frontier near the border of Afghanistan. It is also an Air Force Academy, where undergraduate candidates get training in flying and pass through as flying officers. Graduates then train in Aeronautical and Avionics engineering. It is the Air Force headquarters and one of the largest military garrisons.

Risalpur reflected the major influences of the British Raj. It was one of the very beautiful campuses of the RAF and had flowers growing profusely in the gardens. The officers' mess was a very beautiful building and had vast gardens full of fruit and ornamental trees; it seemed like no money was spared when the British built that campus. The house Shahjahan and family moved into was big, with large gardens around it. Everyone had their own room with attached bathrooms and showers. There was a big dining table in the dining room and all the floors were shiny. Mumtaz had cleaners, dobbies (people who wash clothes), and gardeners. Everyone was delighted and quickly settled in. And even Jack the dog was over the moon and loved the freedom of running around the gardens.

Shahjahan's brother Tariq, who was only ten years old then, had admission into the convent school. The school bus picked him up in the morning and dropped him home in the afternoon. Tariq was to become a very significant person in Naseeb's life. It was Christmas a few months after they moved, and Shahjahan took Naseeb, who was then four years old, to the convent to give Christmas presents to the nuns. Naseeb had never seen a nun before and thought they looked beautiful in their black dresses. She was told that the nuns wore white dresses in the summer. There was a beautiful Christmas tree in the room and this was the first time Naseeb had seen a Christmas tree. She thought this was the most beautiful thing she had ever seen. Mother Dorothy and Sister Anthony gave her sweets from the tree, and Naseeb fell in love with these nuns.

After Christmas, Naseeb also had admission to the convent school. On Naseeb's first day, Shahjahan and Mumtaz took her to school. Naseeb was a bit upset when her parents left, but she soon settled down. After that, she travelled to school with her Uncle Tariq each day, and came home on the school bus in the afternoons. Naseeb loved the beautiful books from Britain that had poems like Jack and Jill, and had colourful photos with lovely pictures of people and houses, and girls in lovely frocks and sandy beaches and blue sky and sea. It all looked stunningly inviting, a huge contrast to what was to come.

On one side of the house there was a kitchen garden with tomatoes, cucumbers, chillies, aubergine, okra, onions, radishes, mint and coriander. Naseeb would spend hours in the vegetable garden and pick the vegetables for her mother. She loved the gardens and the perfume of the flowers, especially roses - there were sweet peas, jasmine, gardenias and many other exotic flowers. She loved the smell of the dry earth when it was watered. Sometimes when she came back from school feeling hot and tired, she would get off the bus and instead of going into the house, she would lie in the flower bed which was cool and perfumed by the flowers and fall asleep there. Her mother would be looking for her all over the place. Sometimes the gardener would find her in the flowerbed, her long black plaits and her uniform covered in mud. Mumtaz was not pleased.

During this time, most of the extended family moved to Rawalpindi. Due to the partition, some Hindu families had left a nearby temple empty, and it had several rooms around the prayer rooms and a big courtyard with pomegranates and jamun trees. The entire extended family moved into the temple. They used every room around the courtyard but never went into the prayer room where they believed the Hindu gods were. It was ironic that a Pir family would live in a temple.

Mumtaz and Shahjahan travelled a lot. Mumtaz took her family to visit her relatives in Rawalpindi every summer and also when there were weddings and funerals. And Shahjahan played hockey all over the country and the world. He played hockey in Australia, New Zealand, Hong Kong, Bangkok and Singapore. When Shahjahan was in Singapore, he stayed with his father-in-law Wilayat Shah, who had left Delhi many decades ago. Shahjahan asked Wilayat Shah why he never went back to his wife and children in India. Wilayat Shah's answer was that he knew his first wife and the rest of the extended family would not let him come back to Singapore and that he did not want to repeat the same mistake he had made with his first family by leaving the second family. He gave Shahjahan lots of silk clothes and expensive jewellery to take back to his daughter, Mumtaz, and his granddaughters, Naseeb and Farah.

The extended family from Rawalpindi and the village Khruli also visited Risalpur and stayed in Shahjahan and Mumtaz's house for weeks. People often visited unannounced. Often Mumtaz would get a message from the guardroom on the gate that there were visitors to be collected. There was always some aunty, uncle, grandfather or grandmother living with the family, but Tariq and one of the aunties lived there permanently.

Once, Mohammed Ali Shah, Shahjahan's grandfather (Naseeb's great-grandfather) visited the family. Her great-grandfather must have been more than seventy years old. Shahjahan and Mumtaz were very fond of him and delighted to have him in their home. Most things which were normal for the family were new to him and he was surprised to see them. For example, he could not understand how various fruits were put in bottles. Ali Shah only saw fruits in their fresh state. Shahjahan took him to the aerodrome to show him various aeroplanes and got him to sit in one or two. Mohammed Ali Shah was surprised and delighted. Shahjahan also took him to an Air Force recording studio. Mohammed Ali Shah recorded his favourite Sufi song and could not believe that he could listen back to his own voice and tears were running down his face with joy. One day, Tariq and Naseeb were asked to take Mohammed Ali Shah to the mosque. On the way, they passed a cinema where there was a matinee show on, so instead of going to the mosque, Tariq and Naseeb took him to the cinema. Mohammed Ali Shah could not understand the black and white film, especially when there was a sea, and the waves were very high, and he put his feet on the seat just in case the water from the sea came at him. When he went back to his village a few weeks later, he had plenty of material to tell stories under the Banyan tree where the people of the village gathered to talk.

In 1953, when Queen Elizabeth's coronation was taking place, the Armed Forces from the Commonwealth were invited. Shahjahan had been an officer for some time and was one of the officers who was invited to the Coronation. He thought that as an Air Force aeroplane was going, he may as well take his immediate family. His plan was to send the rest of the extended family to Rawalpindi for a few weeks until he and his family were back. Mumtaz packed all her valuables and her silk clothes, which her father had sent from

39

Singapore, in very strong boxes with locks. She also asked the carpenters who working on the veranda to make sturdy wooden boxes so that she could leave her things safely in the house.

Naseeb was very excited about travelling with her family and kept asking her father when they were going to London. Shahjahan told her the passports were getting ready and as soon as they were ready, they would leave. Naseeb thought the carpenters who were working on the veranda were making the passports until Mumtaz explained what a passport was. A few days before leaving, the family was vaccinated to travel, which was a requirement of the British Government. On the same night, Shahjahan and the family were invited to a friend's house for dinner. After dinner, everyone was tired and slightly feverish, so they went to bed and fell asleep. When they woke up in the morning, all the things belonging to Mumtaz and her children had gone. One of the servants was also missing. She was from across the border in no-man's-land, the land in between Afghanistan and Pakistan, which did not belong to anyone. The British had left this land un-allocated, like lots of other places in India. The Kabulis who lived in that area were very strong and traditionally proud fighters. They mainly made guns which anyone could buy from them. Police would not dare enter that area, let alone question anyone, so the servant could not be questioned if she had gone there.

None of Shahjahan's things were taken, but Mumtaz was left with only the suit she was sleeping in – even her shoes were taken. Mumtaz was very upset, particularly about the things her father had sent for her. Shahjahan went to town and bought some saris for Mumtaz, and left for London on his own.

A few months later, that servant invited Mumtaz and her family to her wedding in no-man's-land. Tariq, Naseeb and Farah attended the wedding with Mumtaz, who saw all her clothes and jewellery on display as the dowry for the bride. Mumtaz even saw her sewing machine on display. Mumtaz was beside herself with anger and grief, but she was advised not to say anything if she and her children wanted to leave in one piece. In the evening, Mumtaz and the children left on a *thaga* (a horse and a cart with seats in the front and behind) carrying only a live chicken and some uncooked food. This was Shahjahan's share of the food, as a Kabuli tradition was to send food to the missing visitor.

Mumtaz and Shahjahan got involved in lots of social activities in Risalpur. They regularly went to the officers' mess and played cards, and Mumtaz got together a women's hockey team. She also got involved in social work as a volunteer, gave lectures to women about using local products and not putting too much burden on the economy with imports. The children and the house were looked after by female relatives and servants. All in all, they had a very good life.

Once, Mumtaz visited a maternity hospital and Naseeb, who was about seven years old, went with her. When they were returning home, Naseeb asked her mother where the babies came from. Mumtaz told her they came from their mother's belly, but when Naseeb queried this, Mumtaz said, "they just come out." Shortly after that, Naseeb got six children together and made them lie in a row on the floor of the back veranda. She stuffed small cushions or pieces of cloth in their tops and asked them to lie still so she could deliver their babies. This game went on all afternoon while the grown up were taking a siesta. In the evening, a few women came to see Mumtaz because they were very angry and complained about Naseeb. They said that she had been playing vulgar games with their children, pretending that she was delivering their babies. They also said that she had introduced this thing about their bodies, which was too early for their children to learn. Mumtaz was not aware of this and thought Naseeb could not be doing these things, as she was too young to understand it all. Naseeb was listening to this conversation and thought that she was not too young or stupid to understand it at all. She kept quiet and did not speak when the grownups were talking about the children, but she felt her mother was underestimating her.

When Naseeb was eight and both her grandmothers were present, she asked them why her name was Naseeb. They told her the reasons: because she was firstborn and a girl when a boy would contribute more income; because of the costs of marriage and a dowry; and because of the potential difficulties in finding the right husband for her. There was no one of her age in the extended family, so it would have to be someone in the wider circle of the clan. This could be tricky and it depended on whether her potential husband was good or not. They explained that they feared for her karma, her 'naseeb,' as these events didn't bode well for her future. It did not make sense to Naseeb at that young age. She went into the garden and lay in the flower bed, her favourite place, and she thought about it all afternoon. She had recently seen a film actor called Naz and had read in the newspaper that Naz meant 'pride' or 'proud.' She decided that her name would be Naz from then on. She told her parents that she did not like the name Naseeb and that she should be called Naz. The grandmothers had superstitious reasons for not accepting this change of name, but both parents supported Naseeb to adopt this new name. Mumtaz went to her School the next morning and changed her daughter's name permanently. Thu, Naz (as she became), showed early signs of controlling her own destiny, though she was to experience a significant change in her fortune in the future.

As Naz was growing up, there were increasing complaints from the neighbourhood about her. She had long limbs, and she was very tall for her age, so people, including her family, expected her to behave older than her age. When she was twelve, she looked sixteen, and always looking older continued. Naz loved riding her bike all day or she would be in the flower beds resting. If her bike was confiscated, she would take other people's bikes. She would often tear or damage her clothes on the bike. She would go into other people's gardens to steal fruit or pick tomatoes and cucumbers to eat, instead of eating food at home. Being in the sun, her skin got even darker than it already was. She had very long hair in plaits, but it was always unruly, like her behaviour. She was lanky and often clumsy. She would get children together quite often and do drama or dance classes and was blamed for keeping the children out of their homes too late. She was also blamed for leading other children astray. People were always complaining about Naz.

Naz was studying in the convent school where there was co-education and she always felt equal to boys, as she saw no difference. She would take the bike out of the camp where most people did not think it was safe, but she was fearless. Sometimes, if she found someone's horse mule or tanga, she would run away with it. The owners would come and complain to her parents and sometimes they had to pay fines to the owners. She would be grounded for a few days for bad behaviour, but then she would carry on all the same. Sometimes, Mumtaz would be fed up with her and slap or shout at her, but never in front of Shahjahan. He would never raise his voice to the children. He was a very kind and loving father and always believed that Naz, as she was still a child, would grow out of it.

Naz's family, like all Pakistani families, thought religion was important and they would prayer and celebrate all religious occasions. Naz could not understand why the word Inshalla (God willing), Mashalla, or Allah, were spoken so often. She used to ask questions but never got any satisfactory answers. The family was liberal and never judged other people or religions. People from the convent were invited to any family birthdays or Eid. Once, when Naz was about ten years old, a pilot from the aerodrome came to see Shahjahan. The pilot was still wearing a gas mask which was worn when flying a fighter plane. Naz had never seen this before and thought he must be God. She went inside the house and told her father that God was outside asking for him. This was another thing which made everyone angry.

Naz loved her Uncle Tariq like an older brother and best friend. As well as travelling to school together, they would also do their homework together. They went for long bike rides in the wild area on the western border of Pakistan and also to orchards, because Tariq knew Naz liked fruit gardens. They would go to the orchards which had guavas, pomegranates, plums, pears, and many other fruits, on these occasions, with the owner's permission. There was a canal by the orchards where they would swim and have picnics. Often, they would go to the cinema, which was in the Air Force camp. Naz spent a lot of time with Tariq, who used to listen to her and always supported her. She felt he was the one who understood her the most.

Naz's younger sister Farah was totally different to her, in her looks as well as her behaviour. Farah had very nicely cut hair. Naz was the opposite. When Shahjahan was in Australia once, he saw a particular hair style and brought back a photograph. He asked the hairdresser to cut Naz's hair like the one in the photo, but Naz refused to have her hair cut. Farah was obedient and would go straight home from school, never straying. She stayed closed to her mother and father. Farah was always very careful and would refuse to follow her older sister. People were always comparing the two sisters.

The family atmosphere was relaxed and open. Shahjahan would regularly take everyone for picnics with other families and they would have dinner parties. Shahjahan had lots of friends from his military college days, so friends were always visiting them. They would go to a special place called Attak by the river to eat fish. Sometimes they would all go across the border to eat original Balti lamb. Shahjahan would take them to Karachi to see the very big city and to see the sea. They regularly visited ancient and archaeological sites.

Naz's school also went out on trips, and she particularly liked the trips to farms, what the school called nature study. They taught her about the environment and showed how the plants and trees grew and the effect of the trees on the environment. The very first time Naz saw ginger and turmeric growing, she was fascinated. She loved school and her friends in school, her bedroom, and the gardens. So, Naz was brought up in a safe and open environment that helped her develop an independent nature.

In 1960, ShahJahan decided to retire from the Air Force as he was getting older and could not play hockey anymore. He also wanted to start his own business. Naz was completing her high school education and about to take her matriculation exams. Tariq was already in Rawalpindi, about to finish college and join his brother in business, so the family moved to Rawalpindi. Shahjahan set up a showroom on Mall Road in Rawalpindi, at that time the best area in Rawalpindi. The extended family also moved out of the temple and split up due to education, jobs, and marriage, but all of them remained in Rawalpindi. Visits to the village were very rare and only the grandparents visited Keruli.

Shahjahan and Mumtaz got a house on Murree Road near his parents, Hadier Shah and Amina, and his older siblings. The environment and the culture of Rawalpindi were very different, and it was dusty and dirty in comparison to the RAF camp. The people and community were conservative and not open-minded like people in the Air Force. Naz could not go out on her bike because it was not allowed. Though Naz was fifteen, the community thought she was eighteen and she should be in *purdha*. Tariq protested against this attitude, but the elders did not listen to him. By then, Tariq had a motorbike and he would take her out on the Mall road where the atmosphere was relaxed and liberal. They would have ice cream in a café and chat.

In 1961, by the time Naz was sixteen, her mother had five sons and an army of helpers who did the housework and childcare. Mumtaz was good at organising people and was only seen in the kitchen on Eid. Mumtaz was in charge of all the marriages, births and deaths, and in that house, she was the total matriarch.

As Naz was sixteen, families started to visit her family to ask for the hand of their daughter. The boy of the very first family who came for the hand of Naz was a cadet in the Air Force. After staying in their house for a couple of days, they thought they would rather their son married the younger daughter, Farah. Mumtaz refused this request, and they left, never to be seen again. The second family was from their biradari, a boy in the Army who had very good prospects. The first day they came over to visit the family and see the future bride Naz, Naz stole the future groom's bike while Mumtaz and everyone else were busy looking after the guest. It was better than Naz's own bike and she went to visit the extended family who lived in a different part of Rawalpindi. She came home in the evening with dirty and torn clothes, her long hair all over the place and absolutely no idea what was going on in the home. Tariq was looking for her everywhere. The guests had had their dinner and left.

The third family who came were from their distant biradari, and had been recommended by Mumtaz's aunt. Shahjahan had met the prospective groom in a small town where he was working. At the time, he was unaware of any of the negotiations arranging a marriage for Naz. The boy's mother came to visit the family to see the future wife of her son and stayed a few days. This time, Naz was told to stay in and wear decent clothes. Mumtaz and the other women of the family talked, while Naz just sat and listened, totally ignored. The boy was going to England to study and his mother wanted him to get married before leaving. The boy's mother also expressed a wish to marry her son to the younger daughter, Farah. They said Naz was too thin, too tall (she was 5 feet 10 inches then), and had darker skin, whereas Farah had lighter skin, was not too tall, not too thin, and was more ladylike. Mumtaz and the other women said that if the younger one got married first, then they would have problems marrying Naz to anyone. When Naz heard this, rather than feeling sorry for herself, she thought it was great. She would go to university with Uncle Tariq and have a very good time.

Chapter 4

Young Adult

Rawalpindi is a Garrison city and has been since the British Raj. It is the headquarters of the Pakistani army. A large part of the city comes under the cantonment area, which is cleaner and better organised than the rest of the city. There are cinemas which show English and American films, and beautiful cafes and restaurants. All in all, it has a liberal atmosphere. Some remnants of the British Raj remain, like the life size statute of queen Victoria, grand churches, spacious bungalows, and well organised gardens and streets. The area has a number of English-speaking schools, and some British families remained living there after Pakistani independence.

Rawalpindi is called Pindi and the rest of the city is like any other city in Punjab. Families and clans from the nearby villages have always moved to this city for employment and education, and they sell their fruits, vegetables and other seasonal produce in the city's markets. There are lots of street food shops and restaurants, and several bazars big and small.

When Naz was young there were two major colleges – Gordon College and the Government college. Both were built and established during the Raj and are still going strong. The best thing about Pindi is its very close to Murree Hills, so as soon as the temperature rises in Pindi people head towards Murree Hills to cool down.

But after moving to Rawalpindi, Naz was very unhappy as she missed the freedom and safe environment of the Airforce camp. She missed the gardens, the home school, and friends. The home in Rawalpindi was not big enough for all the people living there, plus she had to share her bedroom with her sister and brothers. It was very depressing for her to think that as everyone now thought of her as grownup, she had to learn to cook, wash and do other household chores. Suddenly, from being a child, she had become a woman. There were always too many people visiting the home. Shahjahan and Mumtaz also came under pressure from the biradari and had to adopt a more conservative lifestyle.

The only good thing was that Shahjahan got three newspapers delivered, one in English and two in Urdu, plus weekly women's magazines for Mumtaz and the girls, a sports magazine for Shahjahan and comics for the children. However, when Shahjahan ran into financial difficulty, he stopped being able to pay the newspaperman, but they still kept being delivered. In the end, Shahjahan owed him so much money that instead of giving him the money, he bought a bicycle for the man. Naz and her family loved to read the newspapers and magazines. After breakfast, they would discuss the news and politics. In those days, there was news about President

Kennedy and Jackie Kennedy and her fashions, lots about Marilyn Monroe, indeed publicity about the Profumo affair, as well as the local news and gossip. The elders thought that girls should not be reading the newspapers, that they were getting fancy ideas from reading all those papers, and it should be stopped. But Shahjahan put his foot down with them and did not do as they wanted.

The other good thing was Uncle Tariq. He was a very handsome man, and like other men in the family, was over six feet tall, very graceful, and had long, slender limbs. Sometime earlier, when Tariq and other uncles picked Naz up from school, all the girls and female teachers would pay compliments to Naz about her uncles. Tariq always made everyone laugh with his sense of humour, and he was also kind and very caring.

When Queen Elizabeth came to Pakistan in 1961, Uncle Tariq took all the family to a friend's house where they had a good view of the Queen passing by. He made a day of it, arranging a picnic before they saw the Queen and dinner out in the evening. It was a memorable day with all the family together and they had a lot of fun.

Not long after, Shahjahan and the family had visitors – the woman who had visited a few months previously to arrange her son's marriage and had left his photograph. This time, she came with the son, Yunis. The visitors stayed in their home for a couple of days and Yunis stayed in a room where only men could go – women were not allowed. Similarly, he was not allowed to come into the women's area. There was a lot of commotion in the house and then more family arrived from other parts of Rawalpindi. No one had told Naz anything and unfortunately, her father and Uncle Tariq were out of town.

One of Naz's aunties, Alia, who was only two years older than Naz, and was her best friend, then told her that she would have *Nikah* with Yunis that day. She gave Naz some new shiny clothes to wear and told her to get ready. It seemed like everyone was in a hurry and everything was happening so quickly that no one had time to explain anything to anyone. All she heard was what grownups were saying. Naz was numb with shock. Aunty Alia helped Naz to put on the clothes and a shiny dupatta (a big scarf) to cover her head and some of her face. As soon as Naz was ready, an uncle (one of Mumtaz's brothers) and two other adults, who were also close relatives, entered the room. The uncle was a religious man, and he believed that the sooner girls got married, the better it was for everyone. He persuaded Mumtaz, and other relatives agreed, that they should get on with Nikah before the prospective groom left for Britain. Naz was crying and thought that if her father or Uncle Tariq were there, then they would not be letting this happen. Naz was sitting on her bed with her feet up, her head buried in her knees and her eyes shut very tight. One of the men said something and young Aunty Alia said, "Yes." Then one of the men pushed a form and a pen in front of Naz's face and asked her to sign at a place. Naz never saw the form before or after she signed it. She was then a married woman. It is quite common in Pakistan that someone can have Nikah, the marriage civil contract, first and *Rukhsaty*, moving to the husband's home or consummation of the marriage, at a later date.

That day in June 1961, when Naz married, she had never seen her husband, and he had never seen her. A few minutes after signing the contract, Naz wanted to get out of those clothes but one of her aunties said not yet and took her into their living room where her husband Yunis was sitting on a chair. The Aunty pushed Naz through the door into the living room and shut the door. There was another chair in front where Yunis was sitting. Naz stumbled and sat on the chair next to him. Her face was still covered with her dupatta, and she had her head down very low, still feeling numb. Yunis said hello but Naz did not say anything. There were windows in the living room opening outside and the second thing Yunis did was to ask her to go and shut the windows. Naz said one word, "No." Perhaps Yunis wanted her to stand up so he could look at her, but this did not happen. The next thing Naz did was to leave the room and go into her own room, lock the door and change immediately into her old clothes.

After dinner, when most of the relatives had already left, and as Yunis and his mother were about to leave, Yunis's mother asked if Naz could go with Yunis and stay in a hotel before he left to go to the UK in the morning. Mumtaz refused, saying that Naz's father was not present, so Naz could not be sent away in his absence. Plus, Naz was not prepared for this. Yunis and his mother left and Yunis left for Britain the following morning. Shahjahan and Mumtaz were told at a later time that the reason everything was so rushed was because Yunis was going to study in England and his parents didn't want to send him as a single man. They were worried that he might marry someone local in Britain and never come back to Pakistan. Naz could join him there as soon as Yunis settled down and she could also continue her education.

These arrangements suited Mumtaz. They thought it would be best for Naz to go to college in Britain and live in an open and liberal country. They thought she would be happier. She would enjoy life and studies in Britain and could ride a bike as much as she wanted there. Mumtaz had always tried very hard to get Naz a good education. She thought Naz needed to be independent and a good education would give her the opportunity. At that time, very few people went to work in Britain and not many people knew the working conditions for immigrants there. The only people Naz's parents knew who went to Britain were the people who went for higher education. There was very little news about the changing culture in Britain or about how the economy was faring after the war. Afterwards, it became common knowledge that the Health Minister Enoch Powell was recruiting people from commonwealth countries to come and work in the NHS. People were told that there were posters with Enoch Powell's photo and the words, 'Your mother country needs you to work for the National Health.' This was particularly the case in certain areas of Pakistan where the Pakistani government had recently built a dam, the Mangla Dam. As a result, that area and many villages nearby had been flooded, so those people needed new work and a lot of them went to Britain. Yunis was living in that same area, which is where he got the information about the recruitment to Britain. Sociologists talk about the 'push and pull' theory of migration, the 'push' being people induced or forced to leave the area of origin and the 'pull' being the process that attracts them to a new place, e.g. the opportunity to work and earn good money. Immigrants often think they will return, but rarely do. Yunis never did return to his home country.

Some days later, when all the relatives had left, Tariq and Shahjahan returned home and got the news about Naz's Nikah. They were very surprised and angry. Before he had left Rawalpindi a few weeks earlier, Uncle Tariq had heard the rumours, but did not think it was actually going to happen. He had a heated argument with Mumtaz because he could not challenge Shahjahan, his older brother, but also because it was Mumtaz who had arranged everything. While everyone was standing in the courtyard arguing, Naz put her arms round her Uncle Tariq and cried like a baby. Tariq then took Naz out for an ice cream and talked to her until she calmed down. Uncle Tariq continued to be very angry about the entire situation and had arguments with Mumtaz in the years that followed.

Life became more normal again, but Naz did not go to college. Instead, she helped with the housework and looking after her younger brothers, which kept her busy all day. There were always relatives visiting and staying for days. Shahjahan was busy trying to establish his business and left everything to Mumtaz, who was happy keeping everything under her control. She would not even let anyone buy the meat or groceries because she thought they could not select the things she would choose. She would go herself and take someone with her to carry the shopping. Mumtaz controlled everything. She was very fond of flowers and gardening and was particularly fond of growing flowers called Arabian Jasmine. This is mostly grown in the subcontinent and a very popular perfume, Motia Attar, is made from it. It was traditionally the perfume of the Mughal kings and queens. Due to the lack of a garden in the Rawalpindi home, she had them in big pots. If anyone in the family tried to water the pots and the water ran down the courtyard, she would shout at them for not watering the plants properly.

Shahjahan always woke up in the morning for his prayers before sunrise and before everyone else. He would wash, say his prays and make some tea and boil two eggs. Then he would pick Arabian Jasmine flowers from the garden and put them on Mumtaz's pillow and give her tea and a boiled egg. This was the routine all his life. Every morning after breakfast, Mumtaz would ask Shahjahan what they should cook for the evening meal. Shahjahan would name some food, knowing very well that at the end of the day, Mumtaz would cook what she liked. It was a game in their life which was played for many years. He knew she was just asking as a formality. Naz never saw her father shouting at her mother. If there was any shouting, it would be Mumtaz. There was a tradition then not to call your husband by his name, but Mumtaz defied that tradition too, always calling him by his name. His parents were unhappy about this. Shahjahan and Mumtaz used to laugh and talk a lot, always welcoming visitors and enjoying their company. As a couple, they were very much respected in the biradari and if any important decisions were to be made, people would come to them for advice.

All Naz's brothers went to a nearby school, St Paul's. The owner of the school was a retired Army Captain. He was a very good friend of Shahjahan and everyone in Shahjahan's family called him Captain Sahib. Captain Sahib's wife was Alison, and she was called Aunty Ali by the family. She loved the children and all of Naz's brothers adored her. The two families had a great relationship. They all finished school in St Paul's and later some of their own children went to that school. Some of their biradari who could afford it, also sent their children to St Paul's school.

As Naz did not go to college and as a married person, she lost confidence in being with other students. Farah did not want to go to the new city without her older sister, so Shahjahan and Mumtaz decided to have home tuition for both girls. Shahjahan had another college friend, a professor, who all the children called Uncle Mahmood. He was a very jolly person who knew the family very well and gave story books to the two girls when they were very young. Uncle Mahmood was very keen on girls having education and always said to Shahjahan that the no one would be able to beat your girls at anything. Naz and Farah did not know at that time what Uncle Mahmood meant, but no doubt the parents understood. Uncle Mahmood took the responsibility of teaching both sisters the 'O' and 'A' level syllabi. He was a very enthusiastic teacher and taught the girls how to study and pass exams. During this time, Yunis had started to write letters to Naz from England and gradually the letters became regular. Usually, the letters contained very little information about himself or England, or where he was living. He just asked about the welfare of Naz's family and gave news of his own family in Pakistan. Naz was encouraged by her mother to write back to Yunis and try to get to know him. Naz wrote back to him sometimes, telling him about her private tuition with Uncle Mahmood. Yunis did not show much interest in her studies but instead started to write somewhat romantic letters like "I can't wait to see you" and "come and join me as soon as possible."

Two years went by after the Nikah. The pressure from Yunis's parents to send Naz to join her husband increased. It was decided that, after Naz's exams in April, she could leave for Britain. Her family started the process of getting a passport, but no one had written down her date of birth. However, the family knew the year was when the war ended because they remembered that, as a very small baby, she was carried by her mother to see the Victory Parade. Therefore, the year must have been 1945, and the month must have been May because it was the beginning of summer and certain fruits were in season at the time. In those days, specific dates did not matter much. The registration of the birth of a child did not need to be registered, especially when the baby was born at home. Naz's father discussed the issue of the date of birth with Mumtaz and he chose her date of birth as 1st May 1945. This was the date which stayed with her forever. According to this date, she married when she was sixteen and her husband was thirty-one years old. Naz found out later that no one had asked him about his age at the time.

In June 1963, the passport was ready, and a seat was booked for Naz to fly from Rawalpindi to Newcastle Upon

Tyne via Karachi and London. As usual, the entire biradari got together, with everyone chipping in to do the cooking, packing and looking after the extended family. Everyone felt very depressed and had a heavy heart. Naz herself was wondering what life in the future held for her. Tariq was out of town but had said he was coming back to see Naz off and would buy her a gold necklace to remember him by.

After lunch one day, everyone was lying around, and Naz was lying in bed with her grandmother, Amina. Mumtaz started screaming and beating her breast, saying Tariq was dead. Everyone ran into the courtyard and started to scream and cry. There was a lot of confusion as to what had happened. Shahjahan left the house with some other male relatives to find out what happened. They heard that Tariq was coming back to Rawalpindi on his motorbike, which was a big heavy bike, and had had an accident. He had a collision with a truck coming the other way on the wrong side of the road and was killed immediately. Grandmother Amina and grandfather Hadier Shah were beside themselves with grief. Everyone was crying loudly and had their arms around each other.

A few hours later, Shahjahan brought his younger brother's body home. When Naz saw her soulmate's twenty-two-year-old broken body, she howled like a wounded wolf. As she was touching his beautiful thick black hair, she saw his neck, which had a circle of bruises around it. It seemed to her that he had been wearing the gold chain which he said he would bring for her, and someone had pulled it off his neck. After she saw that, his death and this violation of his body, for her, an earthquake and tsunami came together and she

59

felt she had drowned, pushed deep into the sea. She lost any sense of being for many hours. Tariq was buried that evening according to the religion and tradition where the dead are washed at home, wrapped in a white cotton cloth and buried within a few hours.

Someone from the family went to the post office and sent a telegram to Yunis saying Naz's flight was cancelled due to the death of Tariq. All the women got busy cooking and making cups of tea for the visitors. People were talking, crying, and repeating Tariq's story again and again. Shahjahan and Mumtaz cried a lot. This was the first time that Naz had seen her parents cry like that. There is a traditional mourning period of forty days and there are lots of rituals and traditions for this sort of situation. For example, every family from the biradari takes turns to pay for and cook a meal in the deceased's home to take the pressure off the family. The extended family stays around for days to talk, cry, and pray together.

Naz's in-laws also came to pay their condolences and started to discuss the issue of Naz joining Yunis in Britain. It was agreed that after the forty days, Naz would leave to join her husband.

After a few weeks, most people left and Mumtaz started to prepare and pack clothes, jewellery, and presents for Naz to take with her. Naz was not prepared for this journey, but when she saw her parents were so grief stricken, she did not want to cause any further problems for them.

In September 1963, a seat was booked for Naz to leave home for Britain. All the extended family got together: grandparents, all the aunties and uncles and their children.

Great grandmother Resham Jan, who had come from Kashmir some decades ago, also came. Mumtaz asked Naz to wear loose cotton clothes when she was in the aeroplane so she would be comfortable on the flight. She should then change in London into her bridal red and gold sari and put on her gold jewellery before landing in Newcastle upon Tyne.

Everyone came to the airport to see Naz off. They were all crying except Naz, who was totally numb and could not feel anything or hear anyone. Her heart was sinking, her mouth was dry, and her stomach was feeling very strange. In those days, Rawalpindi airport was very small. You could see the aeroplane from the balcony, which was very close to where the aeroplanes were. They all watched Naz climbing up the steps into the aeroplane. When the door shut and the aeroplane was about to take off, great grandmother Resham Jan cried very hard, rubbing her hands together with grief. She said, "This happened to me once and now the same thing is happening to my great granddaughter. The only difference is that I was on the back of a horse and she is in an aeroplane. I cried all the way to Punjab and I know Naz will be crying all the way too." Resham Jan was right.

Chapter 5

Early Marriage

Naz cried all the way to Karachi, only stopping when she had to get her things together before she landed. After a few hours, she got on a bigger plane to fly to London. On this flight, she sat next to a young woman of a similar age to herself, also from Pakistan. This young person looked relaxed and comfortable in comparison to Naz, who was still very depressed and had a terrible sinking feeling in her stomach. Naz found out that this woman was going to study in Oxford. She had gone through the admission procedure already and would join the college as soon as she got to Oxford. Naz soon realised that the people who travelled to Britain to undertake higher education were very different to herself. This person was not married and looked very different. Her clothes, her shoes, and her perfume were unfamiliar, and Naz realised that this young woman was from a different class. She was going to London because she wanted to, and she would be able to return whenever she wished. Naz compared herself to her companion. As a married woman, it would be up to her husband whether she went to college or not; it would depend on what he wanted. She would not be able to go back home if she wanted to, and this thought filled Naz with dread and fear. The thought of having left everyone back home and going into the unknown felt unbearable.

When Naz went through immigration control at Heathrow, one of the immigration officers asked her to go into a cubicle and strip off. The immigration officer told her that a doctor would come and check her. Naz was very confused and frightened. She had never taken her clothes off in front of anyone before and had to do this in a small cubicle in front of a stranger. The doctor came and checked her breathing and did a lung function test in case she had tuberculosis. Naz had lost a lot of weight due to grief and unhappiness, and she looked quite drawn. This experience added to her trauma, but later, Naz found out that immigration control sometimes also did virginity tests. Somehow, she was spared that humiliation.

The time was running out for her to catch another flight. Her mother had told her to change into her bridal sari and put on all her jewellery before she caught the flight to Newcastle. She started to panic and was running all over Heathrow trying to find toilets to get changed. Luckily then, in 1963, Heathrow was a much smaller airport, and she found a toilet to get changed. As she was halfway through putting on her sari (six metres of cloth!) a caretaker came and chased her out because she was in the men's toilet. Eventually, she got on the flight to Newcastle upon Tyne. As the airport at her destination was very small, a wooden stepladder on wheels was brought to the aeroplane for all the passengers to get off. When Naz went into the reception area, she saw two Asians, a man and a woman. As she was the only passenger on the flight who was Asian, and in a bridal sari, it was easy for these people to work out who she was. Naz got into a taxi with them and went to their house. She could not see the man whom she had married two years previously. She was too shy to ask them about him and they did not bother to tell her, although they could see her anxiety. They only said that they were related to Naz's husband Yunis, and they had two children. When Naz enquired where the children were, they said they were in school. Naz asked if they went to night school as it was quite dark, and she was told that it was only 3 o'clock in the afternoon. This was a shock to Naz because the middle of the afternoon in Rawalpindi was very bright on a sunny day, even in winter. It all looked very depressing.

For two days, Naz lived with these strangers and still no one told her the whereabouts of the man she had married. Naz thought it was strange that no one was communicating. No laughter, no warmth like back home. On the third day, Yunis turned up but didn't bother to explain where he had been. He just told her to get ready as they were leaving, and next thing, they were on a train to Sheffield. On the train Naz was thinking how everything was different – weather, people, lifestyle. It was nothing like she had seen in English books when she was in school. In the books, the sky and sea were blue, and young people wore summer clothes in September. It was nothing like that in the north of Britain. Now that she was here, she thought that she would have to live with it and not bother her family in Rawalpindi anymore. She went very quiet and did not ask questions, nor did she show any interest in anything or anyone. She felt not a bit of excitement or happiness. They did not talk on the train and Naz kept looking out of the window. Everything looked so different and unfamiliar, and cold in every way.

Naz and Yunis got off the train in Sheffield and got on a bus. They went into a small terraced house and went upstairs to a small room. The room had a bed and a very small wardrobe. Naz did not ask any questions but started to unpack and gave Yunis some presents which Mumtaz had sent. In the bottom drawer of the wardrobe there were some women's undergarments. Naz pushed them aside and put some clothes in that drawer and left the rest in her suitcases. She did not talk because she was shy and totally bewildered, and Yunis did not talk because he did not know what to say and because he was not articulate enough to strike up a conversation. Normally in arranged marriages, the couple live with the extended family. They have lots of people to converse with and plenty of opportunities to get to know each other. It was nothing like this in Sheffield.

Soon, it was apparent that this was the only room Naz and Yunis were going to be living in. The other rooms in the house were rented to single men, mostly from Jamaica and the West Indies, and these men were used to sharing rooms with men from a similar background. They worked very hard and long hours and sometimes did night shifts too. There was a tiny kitchen downstairs which was shared by everyone, no bathroom, and the toilet was in the yard, a long way away.

Yunis did not allow Naz to go into the kitchen because there were always men there hanging around smoking. She could only go to the toilet when her husband took her in the morning and at night. They ate white bread and Heinz beans, day in and day out. Yunis would lock her in the room before going to work and unlock the room when he got back from work. Once, Naz was desperate to have a pee and the door was locked, so she peed in his boot and then tried to empty the urine out of the window. The boot fell out on the road and when Yunis looked for his boot, he could not find it. Naz had to tell him what had happened. He was very angry and shouted at her, which was very hurtful. In order to have a bath, or wash clothes, Yunis sometimes let her out. She had to go to the corporation baths, which was a half-hour walk down the hill. Coming back was always difficult, carrying wet clothes and having wet hair. Naz had very long, thick black hair and it would take hours before her hair was dry. Climbing up the hill from the baths reminded Naz of Keruli, where women went to the waterfalls to bathe and wash. Here it was a totally different environment. In Keruli, women went together with their friends and neighbours to the mountains with fruit gardens, and plenty of sunshine and laughter. In Sheffield, Naz was alone in rows of derelict houses, grey skies and in absolute poverty.

On her route back from the corporation baths, when she would be climbing the hill, she had the view of a high-rise building with lights on and young people inside. She worked out that it was a college and that the young people were students of a similar age to herself. To Naz, they looked warm, secure, happy, and confident. She used to stand there and watch them with envy, feeling the complete opposite – cold, insecure, poor, and trapped. That was the future she had hoped for, but it now seemed impossible. The image of these young people studying in a safe atmosphere remained with her for the rest of her life.

Yunis had a request from his family to send them a photograph of him and Naz together. He took her to a photographer's shop, and the photographer tried to position them properly. As they were getting ready for the photo, the photographer touched Naz's hair to bring it forward to show her long hair in the photo and said to Yunis that his wife was beautiful. Yunis became very angry and left the shop without having any photo taken. A few days later, Yunis took her to another photographer's shop. As the photographer was getting ready, Yunis took *surma* (black powder like eye liner that women put on their eyelids to make them look beautiful) from his pocket and started to put it on his eyelids. Naz had never seen any man wearing *surma* before. She asked him not to use it, but he continued and this was the first and the last photo they ever had together.

When this photo arrived in Pakistan, everyone could see how unhappy Naz looked, but no one knew what to do about it. Naz tried to write to his parents about the situation, but every time she wrote a letter, Yunis took it from her and tore it up in front of her. There was nothing she could do about it. Naz did not know how to fight or argue with him, or perhaps she was too insecure to take a risk.

She found out that her husband could only do manual work and was an orderly in a hospital. She later found out that Yunis had had smallpox in childhood and during this time, his arm had become damaged. This had resulted in his arm shrinking, it became stiff from the upper arm to the bottom of his elbow. Therefore, the movement of that arm was very restricted and he could not, for example, bring that arm to his face or make similar movements. Yunis disguised it very well and no one could see this when he was wearing a shirt. Naz had seen the arm but never asked about it. Someone told her much later in life.

Yunis always told her that she was ugly because of her darker skin and that he was very good looking and attractive to other women. Yunis had had relationships with other women before Naz joined him, and this continued throughout their marriage. Once, he took Naz out and bought her fish and chips. She thought this was one of the best things she had ever tasted. That was when they he told her about his relationships with other women. Naz felt nothing and didn't say anything.

Naz was not interested in his relationships. This was the least of her problems. She asked him to buy her a little radio so she could listen to the news. She remembered once when she was five or six years old, asking her father why he read the newspapers and also listened to the news on the radio each day. Her father told her that he also read the newspapers because they had more detail than the radio. Naz thought of this, but buying a newspaper every day was out of the question.

In Pakistani society, people enjoy communicating and

verbalising their emotions and feelings openly and freely. In Naz's family it was even more so. Everyone had a say and could contribute to whatever was going on. For example, when Naz was growing up, although the literacy rate was lower, even the barber, tailor and greengrocer shops had a newspaper for people to read. Early in the mornings, there would often be one person reading the newspaper, and five or six other people listening and discussing the current events politics and whatever was going on in the world. Even now with electronic media access to news and social media, people still communicate and exchange views with a lot of enthusiasm.

In November 1963, when she was listening to the 8am news on BBC radio, she heard that President Kennedy had been shot and had later died. Naz was desperate to speak to someone because, like most people, she was shocked and wanted to share this with someone, as she used to do with her family in Rawalpindi. Yunis was lying in bed and she gave him the news but he just shouted at her and said "What was he to you? Why are you so upset?" Naz was very disappointed and realised that this man was not interested in anything.

As Naz became fully aware of Yunis' behaviour and attitude towards life and other people, she became sad as well as bitterly disappointed. She felt her heart sink like the Titanic. It was bearable to eat white bread and Heinz beans every day and live in one room. These things can be improved, perhaps changed. But to have no-one to talk to, or share bad news or laughter with, was unbearable. Real poverty was not having friends or a community. She could not understand at the time why Yunis had no friends, but looking back, Naz thinks that he was much older than he said he was, despite the fact that he didn't appear to have had much life experience. Or maybe he was depressed. He started to become more critical of Naz, and more bad tempered. He often shouted at her. Naz was not mature or confident enough to argue or handle the situation and she became very quiet. She compared him to her own father and the culture of her own family. For the first time, Naz thought about naseeb or destiny and wondered if this was her naseeb. Was it true that in some cultures, a girl's naseeb was tied up with her husband? If you have a bad husband, does she either have to accept her naseeb? And just hope that he may become good? When Naz thinks about it now, she realises she has seen women waiting for their partner to change or they think they will change him. It seems they are looking for something which seldom happens. Was the idea of naseeb how women were socialised to accept their lot? Naz had been raised to think and question things, and her mother was certainly a woman in control of her life, yet Naz still felt powerless to change her circumstances. What chance did other women have who had less liberal parents? She did not fight back or get angry. It was as if someone had switched off her spirit. Yet, somewhere deep down, she believed things would change sooner or later. She believed that things could not remain the same, and she hoped things would change for the better.

One thing Yunis said to Naz repeatedly right from the beginning was that, as soon as a normal woman got married, she would want to have children. This made little sense to Naz because she had never thought about these things. It made her feel that this was the only reason he had married, especially as he didn't seem to know how to relate to a woman as an equal partner. He appeared very old-fashioned in his ways. Everything he said to her was new and somewhat strange. Soon, Naz was pregnant. In December, three months after leaving home, she started being sick a lot and feeling very tired and weak. She was very unhappy about being locked up in a small room all day and, surprisingly, Yunis also felt that it would be better to move out of that place. They both went looking for another room to rent, perhaps a bigger room this time. They walked the streets of Sheffield looking for a room to rent, but wherever they went, they found a sign saying "No blacks, no Irish, no dogs."

It was a very strange experience for Naz, who experienced rejection and humiliation that no one was willing to rent a room to them. Naz carried on living this lifestyle, eating white bread and baked beans. Sometimes Yunis would bring fish and chips in to share and they would be her best days. Except for the radio, Naz had never asked Younis for anything. She had no expectations of him and she did not show any emotions. She was too young to express any ideas or opinions of her own. All she knew was that this was going to be her life, and she had to adopt this lifestyle. They may one day have their own kitchen where they could cook and have a proper meal.

When Yunis came home each day, he did not talk, laugh, or share his thoughts. If he got letters from Pakistan, he would never share them with Naz or show any emotions.

He was always very tired and quiet. This was very hard for Naz. He did not have any friends, nor did he try to make any, and he certainly did not encourage Naz to make friends. Naz had no-one to talk to about her family and friends in Rawalpindi.

The other thing which was very depressing for Naz was the image in Yunis's head of what a good wife should be. The only thing Naz could understand was that Yunis thought a good wife should be subdued, passive, and not ask questions. He also wanted his wife to be dressed in a shiny sari, wearing all her jewellery, and possibly smiling. Naz had never heard such things, and she was not going to be dressed up all day sitting in the room. In comparison, Naz had an image of a husband who was like her father Shahjahan, who always thought of his wife as an equal partner, was always warm, talking, sharing, and laughing, the same as her uncle Tariq. Naz's father was a lot of fun and sometimes he would have races in a rubber dingy with his friends. They would start from up the river and end up at the bottom, where all Naz's family and the families of Shahjahan's friends would be waiting, ready to have a barbecue. Naz and all the children were taken to watch football and if cricket was playing in Rawalpindi, the family would go and have a picnic there. She remembered that when they all went for picnics, they would explore new places and have meals at other people's homes or people would go to their homes and eat together. The concept of eating alone was thought of as a curse; food should be shared.

It was apparent Yunis had very narrow life experiences

as well as a very different way of family living. Though Naz never asked him, it was clear that he had very little education and had no intention of getting any more education. Naz understood there was no question of her having any more education herself, or a job for that matter. Yunis lacked confidence and any ambition to move forward in life. There was nothing Naz liked about Yunis. He looked very different from all the men she knew in her family. This included his looks as well as his character. She was also angry about the deception and pretence that had taken place. Naz came from a family where people were honest, trusting and sincere. However, there was no question of Naz leaving Yunis and going back to Pakistan, especially as she was pregnant now. Yunis would never allow this to happen.

In the 1950s and 1960s, people in India and Pakistan knew very little about Britain, particularly its social and economic conditions and about the circumstances in which people lived. Quite often, people had no connections in Britain who could pass back information about living conditions there. Usually, single men with little education came first and did labouring in the hospitals and factories. Some who went back to the sub-continent to look for a wife were deceptive and never told the whole truth. If reports did get back home, they would always involve exaggerated stories of affluence and rich living. It is said that wherever the immigrants went, this was often the case. People who leave their country for the betterment of themselves and their families don't like to admit to any hardship or humiliation but give the impression of success. This was another reason Yunis did not want Naz to write back and tell her family the real situation.

Naz did not think there was any other alternative. Leaving him or divorce was unheard of in her family, as this would have brought shame to the family's reputation. Instead, she tried to adjust herself to the situation. Her personality changed, at least it appeared so from the outside; she looked very unhappy and trapped in a situation out of which it seemed impossible to leave. She thought that after the birth of the child, Yunis might relax a bit and also she would be busy with the baby.

Sometimes, she wondered where her inner strength and this belief came from. Even in the depths of despair, she believed that things could not remain the same. It could not remain this bad forever. She knew this was not normal and that most people could not live like this for too long. Perhaps if she had come from a different type of family, she might have thought differently. But because Naz had very good memories of loving and warm relationships, she had tasted freedom and had trust in the family. She knew that it was possible. Her basic education was in a convent, where women were running a big institution side by side with men. The fearless and courageous training given by the nuns was buried deep in Naz somewhere. She believed life would not always be like this and the day would come when it would change. She would think like this but could not share it with anyone, not even on paper.

Meanwhile, Yunis' bad temper was getting worse. He shouted and sometimes slapped and kicked Naz, who could not protest. All she could think of was that when Yunis was old, she would still be young and then she could have her own back. But she knew that was fantasy, not a reality.

Naz was on her own one day coming from the corporation baths, when she passed a television shop and she stopped to look at a television. She saw The Beatles singing 'She loves you, yeah yeah yeah'. Her heart just lifted like magic; she thought she was flying with them. Those boys were a similar age to herself, with long hair and she had never heard or seen anything so beautiful and as fantastic as The Beatles. She stood in front of the shop window with wet hair and wet washing and watched them. When they finished, Naz was still in a trance, and she skipped all the way home.

Chapter 6

Glasgow

It was getting more difficult for Naz to live in one room, and she was becoming weak with malnutrition. Yunis became concerned about this, so he decided to move to Glasgow. He had a relative there who owned a one bedroomed flat. Yunis thought he and Naz could go there and share the flat with this relative, Saleem.

In March 1964, when Naz was six months pregnant, she and Yunis took a train to Glasgow without informing Saleem. They took a bus from Glasgow station to the address where Saleem lived, but when they arrived, he was not at home, so they sat on their suitcases outside the building and waited.

While they were waiting, Naz looked around the place, which was even more derelict and run down than the flat they had left in Sheffield. The area in Sheffield was bad enough, but this area in Glasgow was even worse. They were slum tenements, seemingly made of black sandstone (sandstone that had become black with smoke). There was rubbish lying in the street and the people who passed by looked poor. The children who were playing in the street were unwashed and wearing ill fitted shoes and clothes. All in all, it was a depressing sight. Naz was sitting on the suitcase in her flimsy shalwar kamiz and totally inappropriate sandals with no socks. After a while, the children gathered round them and started to shout, "Darkies! Darkies!" At first, Naz had difficulties understanding the Glaswegian accent but later she realised that what the children were shouting was an insult. She felt very embarrassed and frightened.

It was getting dark and very cold. Naz was also hungry and tired. Eventually, Saleem turned up. When he saw Yunis and Naz sitting outside the flats on the suitcases with all the children gathered round them, he became very angry and started to shout at the children. He also cursed and shouted at Yunis and Naz for arriving from Sheffield without asking or informing him.

Eventually, Saleem took Yunis and Naz through the open shared entrance of the tenement, called a 'Close', along a dark stone corridor and up stone stairs to the third floor. The tenements had no ground floor and three upper floors, each with two flats. Each Close had a number (not a name) starting from No 1, which preceded the floor, 1up, 2up and 3up for each floor, and then the flat number. So, for example, an address could be 1,1up, flat number. The corridor and stairs were very badly lit. Often a drunk or a homeless person was sleeping on the floor at the entrance of the tenement. Saleem's flat had two rooms. One room seemed to be the bedroom. The other room, presumably the living room, had no furniture. There was also a small bathroom and a kitchenette in the corridor. Yunis bought a bed to put in the living room, and this is where they slept.

Naz was pleased to get into the flat and use the toilet and she was also pleased to see the kitchen so she could cook proper food. They quickly settled into the flat. A few days later, Saleem found a job for Yunis, so there was a bit of money coming in to buy food. Yunis bought some groceries from a Pakistani shop and Naz cooked the food for everyone, which made them all happy. Yunis was happy to have homemade food. Saleem worked long hours, but Naz always cooked enough for him to eat whenever he was around or saved the food for him to eat later.

One day, Yunis took Naz for a bit of an outing to see a film, and later, eating her usual Pakistani food made her feel happy and normal and settle down a bit. Things seemed to be getting better. Nevertheless, there was still no one to talk to or listen to, and no books or newspapers, which made her sad. However, the thought of having a child filled her with hope and perhaps having a better future.

Yunis suppressed his old-fashioned expectations of what a good wife should be, a bit, and Naz felt relieved and more relaxed with fewer demands on her as a wife. She felt happier wearing her cotton shalwar kamiz, rather than silky shinny cloths that Yunis preferred. He had a manual job, so he was working very long hours for very little money. He never told Naz where he worked or gave her any contact details. Naz asked Yunis for a second-hand sofa and some material and she spend months re-upholstering the sofa, which she had never done before. Working on a project like this gave her a lot of satisfaction. So, they had a bed and a sofa in the living room in a one-bedroom flat. Sometimes, when she wanted to be on her own, she would lie on the sofa. Things were going okay and Yunis even took Naz for a check-up at the antenatal clinic.

On 13 August 1964, when Yunis was at work, Naz went into labour. She went downstairs to the street and rang for an ambulance from a telephone booth. After giving her address to the ambulance staff, Naz went back to the flat and left a note for Yunis before she left in the ambulance. She had very little to take with her to the hospital – the Royal Infirmary – and felt totally alone. She thought about what it was like for women to give birth in Pakistan with so many other people there to support them. She gave birth to a boy. He was the most beautiful baby, and she was filled with pleasure. The baby had very thick black long hair, but he came out with all his face scratched from his long finger nails. The nurses in the hospital started to call him Hamish – a Scottish name – which Naz didn't mind. Later, he was called Raza, but Naz often called him Hamish. The baby was looked after by the nurses, who showed Naz how to carry the baby and how to breast feed.

Though Naz's mother had lots of children, the older children, especially the girls, Naz and her sister Farah, were often sent away to live with the grandparents for a while. So, Naz was never involved in looking after very small babies or had never been anywhere near when her mother was giving birth. In Pakistan, then, and to a certain extent even now, childbirth or pregnancy is not discussed and is often kept hidden from the members of the family. Nothing was discussed in front of the children, so Naz only found out her mother had had a baby after it had happened.

In Glasgow, Naz was in a big maternity ward with the baby in the cot next to her. Nurses were very helpful in showing Naz how to take care of the baby. At visiting time, all the visitors came into the ward to see their babies. Naz could see some visitors were looking at her and wondering why this young woman was on her own. Some visitors would feel sorry for her and share their fruit and flowers with her. In the evening when all the visitors had gone, all the women in the ward and nurses would have fun, like telling jokes, singing and playing games. Though Naz did not understand the Glaswegian accent, she joined in and enjoyed the company of the women and had fun with them.

Three days later, Yunis came to the hospital. He did not bother to explain why it took him three days to come and visit her, nor did Naz ask any questions. Yunis was pleased to see the baby and told Naz to get ready as they were going home. The nurses wrapped the baby and handed him over to Naz. Naz felt very strange as, on the one hand, she was delighted to carry the baby, but on the other, the thought of taking on the responsibility of another human being was very scary. The thought of looking after the baby without the support of nurses was overwhelming. Naz said thank you to the nurses and said goodbye. They left the hospital and took the bus home.

After a couple of days at home, Naz felt lonely and

started to get very depressed. Yunis was at work most of the time and when he did come home, he would eat and go to bed. One day, she felt very strange, like her head had become a brick, so she put the baby in the cot and walked out of the door. She walked towards the railway station to throw herself under the train. The train station was a long way, and she had no idea what she was doing, but she kept walking. When she reached the station, she saw a train and got on it. There were very few people on the train and she just sat there in a trance, looking out of the window, even when it was dark. It seemed like a very long journey. The train went all the way to London and then returned to Glasgow. Naz just stayed on it. She did not speak to anyone, and she didn't eat or drink anything. No one asked her for a ticket or spoke to her. In any case, she did not have any money or anything to sell. The train stopped at Glasgow station; she got out and walked back home.

Naz was away from home for about 48 to 50 hours and when she got back, Yunis was furious and started to shout at her. He did not think of asking Naz the reason she left home. She stayed quiet, and she did not have the courage to tell him how she was feeling. She was also very frightened. Yunis started to hit her with his shoes and then he kicked her. Naz took the beatings without any protest and even had to apologise before he stopped. Yunis accused her of running away with a man and asked Naz who he was and what was his name, Naz did not try to explain to him what happened because she herself did not know what had happened. How could she have explained the last 50 hours?

During the time Naz was away, Saleem and Yunis were

going round the Asian community, asking for Naz. Within twenty-four hours, the entire Asian community knew that Naz had run away with someone and had left her newborn baby at home. Naz already had no friends or family around, so this rumour alienated her even further from the community. If Naz bumped into any Asian women, they would change direction to avoid bumping into her. Naz tried to talk to some women, but no one was willing to listen or understand that she (as she later learned) had postnatal depression. At that time, there was very little awareness of this condition, even in medical circles.

In immigrant communities, women mostly married within their families, so either they knew their husbands before marriage, or they had already married in Pakistan and lived there for a while before coming to Britain. Some already had family or friends in Britain before they joined their husband. None of this was true in Naz's case. Although Yunis was from the biradari, no one from Naz's immediate family knew him. Also, there were no family or friends in Britain who could be a support system for Naz and her baby. The personality and the life experiences of Naz and Yunis were very different. She came from an outgoing family who mixed with a variety of people and trusted strangers. Yunis was the opposite of this, and even having a baby did not change him. He remained the same – he was very tired most of the time, quite bad tempered, suspicious of strangers, and had no friends.

It has been well documented that the early immigrants who first came to Britain found life very tough. They had to do menial jobs that local people did not want to do.

They had to work long hours for very little money, often doing shift work and overtime to make up for low wages. All this, and experiences of racism such as not be able rent places to live, or being denied opportunities for a mortgage, created considerable pressure. There were also other financial pressures. Sometimes immigrants were also supporting older parents or other members of the family in the country of origin. Some had borrowed money to travel to Britain, which they had to pay back within a certain period. All this made some men very depressed and sometimes it was manifested in domestic violence. Of course, this was not all immigrant men, but certainly some. But despite the pressures, there is no excuse for abuse. In the 60s and 70s, women from the subcontinent were often vulnerable due to isolation, lack of education, lack of community support, and the lack of legal protection.

Despite her depression and running away, the situation settled a bit and Naz was happy with the baby, who was developing his own personality. She enjoyed washing him, dressing him, and cooking for everyone – and it was a period of calm. But Naz knew nothing about family planning and didn't think about whether to have more children, and when Raza was six months old, Naz was pregnant again. She started to panic. She felt trapped by their small living space and felt weak and helpless again, but there was nothing she could do. Yunis was happy. It seemed like this had been his plan all along and the reason he had married. Otherwise, there was no warmth or emotional attachment between Naz and her husband. He enjoyed being with his son and showed love for him, but was still restrained to a certain extent.

Yunis had saved four hundred pounds during this time and he bought a flat downstairs so they lived on the level down from Saleem's flat – 2up. This was a one bedroomed flat again with two rooms, one room with a cooker, a sink and two chairs, and one room with two beds. Baby Raza was happy. Yunis bought him toys, and everyone felt they were lucky to have their own place.

In October 1965, Naz gave birth to another son, Omer. This time, the delivery was at home, with the district nurse in attendance. Yunis was in the kitchen holding the toddler while the second baby was born. After the birth, the midwife seemed to be in a hurry and left. Naz's clothes were all wet and dirty, so she called Yunis to fetch clean dry clothes for her. He was in a bad mood because he had been looking after Raza whilst Naz was giving birth and refused to help her. An hour after giving birth, Naz got up, cleaned herself and put on dry clean clothes. She changed the bed and breast fed the newborn baby.

In those days, there was a government grant that provided for baby equipment, so they bought a second-hand pram. Naz liked to take the children out to the nearby park, but sometimes, by the time she finished the housework and got both babies ready and out of the building, she was exhausted. She had to take the pram down two floors first, then take one baby down and leave him in the pram, making sure no one was lurking in the corridor. Then she had to go back up to the flat and take the other baby, and the blankets, down to the pram. If the weather changed and they could no longer go out, she would have to do everything in reverse.

Once, when Naz went through the same routine to take the children out, as soon as she came out with the second baby and the blankets, she realised that she had locked herself and the children out. She started to panic, but did not know how to contact Yunis. Naz remembered a woman whose husband was a friend of Saleem and who had a baby about the same age as Naz's children. She would have nappies and milk for the children. Naz went to her house and told her what happened. Naz borrowed a pen and a paper from the woman and put a note through the door for Yunis. She explained what had happened and where she was and said that whatever time he got home, could he please come and collect the children and Naz. Yunis didn't go to get them and in the end, Naz had to ask the woman if she and the children could stay overnight. The woman very kindly gave them a bed, food for Naz and milk for the children. The next day when Naz and the children went back home, Yunis was very angry and did not speak to Naz and the children for over a week.

It was very hard for Naz to live like this in a confined space, with two very young children, and no support from her husband. She got more and more tired and depressed. Yunis earned very little money for the food and other essentials needed for the family. Moreover, his bad temper created a toxic atmosphere. Naz felt desperate to be able to sit down and talk with Yunis, just like her own parents did, but both Naz and Yunis lacked the art of communication. This lack of trust and confidence made it very hard to work things out.

One of the reasons Naz did not have the confidence to talk was because she was frightened in case he lost his temper and became violent. Not even the children made any difference to that. They were both trapped in a relationship which was not going anywhere; there was no love or even any warmth in the marriage. They both knew that they could not get out of it because of family traditions and constraints.

Chapter 7

Rawalpindi

Naz's parents knew that she had experienced some kind of postnatal depression after the first baby was born and they became very anxious when they heard of the second baby. They were desperate to see Naz and the children. For Mumtaz and Shahjahan, they felt they had lost two of their older children, Tariq and Naz, within few months of each other. They promised Yunis that if he allowed the children to visit Pakistan, they would send her back as soon as he wished. Naz's parents were paying for her and the children to visit them and she was delighted. She thought it would give her a break to think things through and work out her options.

For Naz divorce was not an option. No-one had been divorced in the entire clan. It would be difficult to explain to the biradari that Yunis and Naz had had different up bringings and had different value systems. Naz wanted to have a good education and take up a professional job, whereas Yunis wanted to open a small shop, possibly with Naz and the children working in it too, to save money. No-one in the biradari would understand, because it is the woman who is expected to conform to the man's wishes. The biradari already blamed her parents for sending Naz to a school with English education, taught by Nuns. In the present circumstances with Yunis, she could not have got a reasonable job to earn a decent living. However, there were no adult education colleges in Rawalpindi at that time, so staying there to further her education was also not an option. She didn't want to remarry and anyway, it would be hard to marry in the biradari as a divorced woman with two children. She was very happy to be going back to her family home in Rawalpindi with her two very young children in 1966, but there were many unresolved issues that were still to be faced.

As they got off the plane at Rawalpindi airport, the sunlight was so bright that the children could not open their eyes. The entire family was at the airport to receive them. Naz could not believe how much her brothers had grown since she last saw them – they were very tall and slender. Her mother had a room ready and some cotton clothes for Naz and the boys. It was a relief to wear light and very loose clothes she was comfortable in.

All the grandparents were there, and everyone fell in love with the children, who enjoyed the attention of all the people. Naz was very happy to eat familiar food and be able to communicate with her family and friends. But she did not disclose Yunis's attitude and behaviour towards her and all the problems in her marriage. She had internalised the oppression and started to believe that she was the reason that she had not settled with her husband, that it was her fault. Yunis had repeatedly drummed into Naz how a good wife should behave, and no matter what Naz tried to do, he was never happy. Naz thought that no one would believe her, and the lack of communication and loneliness had exacerbated the situation and Naz's state of mind.

As far as Naz knew at the time, no one else in the family had experienced similar issues as no one had married outside the family and no one had left the country before at such a young age. Later, she found out that her great grandmother had had a similar experience, but she knew nothing of that then. It was always expected that a woman would adopt her husband's values and practices. But especially for Naz, who had strong values, and who had experienced a different family upbringing, she found it hard to accept her husband's way of life. During this first visit, Naz thought that after she had rested and recuperated in Pakistan, she would go back to Yunis. The children would be older and she would also have had time to think, so things would be alright. No one in the family suspected that anything was seriously wrong. There were questions about why Naz had not continued her education, as was agreed before the marriage, but she had a very good excuse, bringing up the children.

The opportunity to travel back to Pakistan was a blessing, and during almost ten years of marriage, Naz would come to spend more than six years in total with her parents. Naz and the children were happy during these times. Shahjahan loved his grandchildren, and they went out regularly. He had a Chevrolet car and he would tell everyone to get ready after the morning prayer before sunrise, to leave home for outings or to visit friends and family before it got too hot. Everyone would pile into the car, singing and chatting all the way. There were always people staying at their home and the children learned to share their food, toys, and their bedroom with other children and adults. At the same time, Naz was gaining confidence and her independence again.

In June, when the temperature was very high in Rawalpindi, Shahjahan rented a house in Murree Hills, a summer place in the mountains established during the British Raj. The entire family moved there until September, when Naz's brothers had to go back to school. Other relatives also visited and sometimes stayed for days. In the evenings, some members of the family would go for walks and take the children with them.

People from all over the country go to Murree Hills. Some spend the whole summer there, some go for a few weeks, and lots of people go for a day trip. All the traders go there to exhibit their goods and the local people sell their dry fruit and fresh fruit to make as much money as possible. Similarly, the restaurants and street food do very good business in the few months of summer. Artists go there to show their paintings or other types of art and music or dancing. Every year there is a book exhibition with lots of new books and writers introduced. The centre of the town is closed to traffic, so people walk up and down on the Mall Road. People meet and greet in the centre and show off their new fashion, their clothes, hairstyle, or their handbags. It seems like anyone and everyone comes out in the evening and quite often Naz would come across her old friends from school. This was the only place in the1960s and 1970s where people would go in the summer. Since then, several places have opened, especially in the Northern areas, where people go in the winter to ski as well as in the summer to escape the heat further south.

When Yunis heard that Naz was freely going to places and enjoying herself, he started to write letters pressurising her to stay at home in pardah and not go to places with friends and family. He thought Naz was out of control and doing whatever she liked. It never occurred to Yunis that his children were happy, and that it was important for them to grow up as happy and loving people.

The last straw for Yunis came the following summer when the entire family, including the grandparents, Naz and the children, went to Murree Hills again. In the middle of the summer, some members of the family had to go back to Rawalpindi, but Naz stayed there with the children and an auntie and her uncle. When Yunis heard that Naz was staying in Muree Hills and her parents were back in Rawalpindi, he was furious and demanded that Naz go back to Glasgow.

Naz returned to Rawalpindi and after a few months, in February 1968, she travelled back to Glasgow. She had been away for one year and ten months. Raza was three and a half years old and Omer, two years, four months.

When Naz went back to Glasgow, this time she had more confidence. She was able to argue with Yunis and she was not prepared to accept unreasonable demands from him. Yet, she still believed that there was no alternative way for them to live. The shame of being divorced was not a real alternative. Somehow, she felt the only way to go on was to stay married and find ways to live with this relationship. She never saw any alternative except to run away and go back to Rawalpindi. But even there, she felt ashamed about her secret and guilty about not being able to settle in her marriage. She was made to feel that it was her responsibility to keep the marriage going. It was a fight/flight situation, but she could do neither of these. She could not fight with Yunis, and with two children and no education, she had no means to take flight. She felt helpless. After a few months back in Glasgow, Naz was pregnant with their third child.

Most of the immigrants who came to Britain in the early 1960s were not very well educated. They planned to earn enough money in Britain to go back to their respective countries and start a business or buy land to start farming, but unfortunately, this rarely happened. Due to the poor wages and the expensive living conditions in Britain, they did not earn enough money to save. Some immigrants sent their wives and children back so that they could save more money. Others never brought their families to Britain in the first place and had relationships with local women, only visiting their home country periodically. Sometimes they had children in both. So very few went back, and often those that did only went back in boxes.

Yunis began to think that the only way he could save money and go back to Pakistan to start a small business was if Naz and the children went back to live with her parents. So, just a couple of weeks before Naz gave birth to her third child, she flew back to Rawalpindi with the two children.

Everyone was happy to see the children. Naz, accompanied by her mother Mumtaz, booked into a maternity hospital. Everyone was hoping for a girl this time as there were already seven boys in the house, five of Naz's brother aged seven to sixteen and Naz's two sons, four and five.

On January 23, Naz gave birth to a baby girl, later named Rumi, and everyone was delighted. Mumtaz was in the hospital with Naz and took her home after a couple of days. This time, there were no postnatal symptoms. Naz looked and felt very healthy. There was lots of joy and celebrating, and the boys could not have enough of this new baby in the family. They all wanted to carry her and pass her round to each other. Naz was worried in case they dropped her and accidentally harmed her, but she became everyone's baby, shared and cared for by all.

Naz's sons Raza and Omer had strong Glaswegian accents, and no one understood them in the beginning, but soon they started to speak Urdu and Punjabi. Naz enrolled them into the local English school. She would take the boys to school in the mornings and bring them back in the afternoons. There was no problem with babysitting, as Naz could go out of the house and it would be understood that other members of the family would automatically take care of the children.

After the boys went to school, Naz had all day to spend with her family and friends. There was always something going on in the biradari, like a wedding, engagement, birth. Naz's family was the only family to have a telephone in the area and if someone had an emergency in the neighbourhood or had to pass on a message, they would ask to use the phone. The house the family lived in was opposite Gordon College, Rawalpindi, which is a famous college in Pakistan. The young men who were studying at the college were members of various different political parties, and so were always physically fighting with each other. Often, they came over to the house bleeding, and asking if they could call the police on the phone. A few years later, Naz recognised some of them when they became ministers in the government. Her family was the first one in the neighbourhood to have a television and at that time, there was only one television channel which would start at five pm. All the children from the area would gather in the middle courtyard and the children would sit on a rug on the floor. Then someone would bring the television out, and they would all watch The Lucy Show or Star Trek.

Naz would tell her mother that this was the best time in her life, but her mother could not understand why Naz thought like that. Naz now had the freedom to do anything she wanted, and she wanted to do something! She thought of working outside the home, which no one in the family had done before. Her first preference was to study further, but that was not possible in Rawalpindi because there was no adult education system. There is now an Open University in Rawalpindi, but this did not exist at the time.

No one in the family wanted Naz to work, but she was offered a job in a library and persuaded her mother and father to let her do the job. They thought she was working for money, but it was very little money and she mostly wanted to do something with her time. It was a very interesting job, buying very old manuscripts from Afghans and other people from central Asia. Men from Afghanistan and Central Asia would bring ancient manuscripts written in Arabic or Persian, mostly written with paints made from the ground powder of differently coloured precious stones like turquoise. These men would bring big bundles of books tied up in a big piece of cloth or sometimes wrapped in their headgear. The books were all very dusty, often damaged, and sometimes incomplete. The most interesting things were the books on old methods of treating various illnesses with herbs and other natural remedies. The sellers were totally unaware of the value of these books, which they found in caves, old houses, or sometimes in skips or rubbish tips. Sometimes, the books were bought by weight. Naz's work also involved very hard and painstaking work separating each page to begin restoring them. But the dust and the gas that came from the books made Naz very sick and she left the library after a few months.

Four years passed and Naz's children were growing up and asking questions about their father. Naz's brothers were becoming teenagers and had their own issues, like their education and relationships outside the family. Her parents were getting older and Naz started to think about her children's future. During those years, Yunis wrote five or six letters and gave no indication about his future plans. One day, friends of Naz's parents, a husband and wife, came to stay with the family. The couple were both journalists and very well educated. The woman had a long conversation with Naz about her future and that of her three children. She questioned Naz about what was going to happen with the children growing up without their father and about when her parents were no longer around to pay for the upkeep of her children. The friend said that at the end of the day, it was their father's responsibility. Naz's parents and the rest of the family were happy for Naz and the children to live with them until Yunis returned to Pakistan. Likewise, the children and Naz were happy to continue living with the extended family. But they all knew that it was an uncertain future. No one knew what plans Yunis had or what he was thinking, but they needed to know what the future might hold.

After the conversation with the guests, Naz wrote to Yunis asking about his future plans, but he never replied. Naz talked to her parents and asked them to pay for her and the children to return to the UK. Shahjahan and Mumtaz were sad to see the children go but they thought in the long run it would be better for the children to be with their father. By this time, Yunis had moved to Newcastle upon Tyne and Naz planned to leave Rawalpindi to return to return to him at the beginning of January 1973. At that time, Raza was nine, Omer was eight, and her daughter Rumi was four. Naz sent a telegram to Yunis informing him of their arrival. He sent a telegram back saying ungraciously, 'you are not welcome,' but it was too late. Naz had already left Rawalpindi with her children.

Naz arrived in a very cold and very grey Newcastle in January 1973 and went to Yunis's address, which was a small shop. He was standing in the shop behind the counter with a woman who Naz later found out was his girlfriend. When Yunis saw Naz and the children standing in the door, he started to shout, telling them to go back to Rawalpindi. This time, Naz was older and had much more confidence than ever before and she told him she had not travelled with three children all the way from Rawalpindi to return. She saw the stairs going from the shop to the flat upstairs, so she took the children and her luggage and went up into the flat.

Chapter 8

Newcastle Upon Tyne

The very small flat above the shop was dark and cold. There were two small rooms and a little kitchenette in a small hallway. Both rooms had a double bed in them. Naz put all her luggage and the children in one of the bedrooms and then went downstairs to the shop to get some food. She cooked the food and fed the children, and she slept in the double bed with the children. In the middle of the night, she woke up and went downstairs to the shop, where she saw a phone. She rang her parents to inform them about her safe arrival and did not tell them anything else. After the phone call, Naz raided the shop, taking bread, butter, jam, eggs, potatoes and fish fingers. When Yunis woke up the next morning, oblivious to the raid in the shop, he started again to demand Naz went back to Rawalpindi. He told her to ask her father to send plane tickets. Naz repeated that she was not going back and that the children were his responsibility. After breakfast, she took the children to be enrolled at a local school, and prepared them to start their new school the next day.

Naz had matured in the time that she had been away and had gained much confidence and courage. She had no feeling for Yunis and all she wanted to do was settle down and get a good education for the children. She was not concerned about Yunis' girlfriend. She only wanted Yunis to take responsibility for the children and take some interest in them. The only topic of conversation he had with Naz was to demand she went back to her parents in Pakistan. Naz would go downstairs every night and raid the shop to bring back food, chocolates and sweets for the children. She was not sure whether Yunis was aware of the stuff missing from the shop. He would leave his bedroom every morning to go to the shop and go to bed after closing the shop. He did not show any interest in the children, and they missed all the attention they were used to from the extended family they had left behind in Rawalpindi. It was Rumi's fourth birthday at the end of January and Naz had a £1, so she bought a very small doll for her.

One morning in March, when Yunis was going downstairs to the shop, he had the tray from the till in his hand, which had lots of money in it. As Naz was very tall and strong, she stood in front of Yunis and asked for some money for the children to buy warm clothes and other necessities. Yunis became abusive as usual and told Naz that she could ask her father to pay for all they needed and for them to go back to her family, as he could not afford to keep them there. By this time, Naz was furious and without thinking of the consequences, she kicked the tray of money, which went everywhere. Yunis picked up the broom and started to hit Naz uncontrollably. She fell to the floor and Yunis kept hitting her on her head. When Yunis thought Naz could not get up, he picked up his money from the floor, locked the flat from the outside, and left. All three children were watching this and screaming. Naz's head was bleeding very badly, and she opened the window, which overlooked the road, and started to shout for help. A couple of people did pass on the road, but when they saw Naz bleeding, they just walked away.

The blood from her head started to come out even faster and her very long hair was dripping with blood. She opened the window again and without thinking of the danger; she walked onto the window ledge to the next-door neighbour's window, where she saw a couple having their breakfast. When they first saw Naz, they were very frightened, seeing this tall thin woman with long black hair dripping with blood and hanging onto the window ledge. However, they opened the window and pulled her into the room. By that time, Naz had lost a lot of blood and she passed out. She came round in the General hospital to a nurse asking her if she had been under a truck in an accident. Naz did not know how to reply to the question.

Though Naz and the children never talked about it at the time, she knew her children would always remember their mother getting violently hit by the broom. Naz's son later reminded her that it was not just an ordinary broom, but one used to clean the yard. In 1973, domestic violence was not recognised by law, and no one wanted to interfere in family violence. It was just called a 'domestic' and no one interfered in domestic problems. Therefore, no one questioned Yunis about having almost killed Naz. There were not many places for women and children to stay away from the family home and the places that did exist were in very poor condition and unsafe.

The main theory discussed in professional circles at that time about violence by men to their partners was about control and power. In terms of immigrant men, it is suggested that they lose power and control due to racism and exclusion, so they take it out on the family, particularly their wives. This may be partly true in some cases, and issues of power and control certainly take place, but not all immigrant men treat their families badly. Women are also abused by men in all types of classes and communities. Issues of misogyny and abuse of women by men are complex and continue to happen, whether it is on the street, in the park, or in the home.

When Naz became conscious in the hospital, she asked for her children. A policeman came and told Naz that he would bring the children to the hospital and told her that his advice was to not go back to her husband, as he may kill her the next time. He brought the children to her and took them all to a women's refuge. Despite the prevailing attitudes and law at the time, this policeman was an empathetic human being and very helpful to Naz. He could see the danger that she was in.

Unfortunately, the women's refuge turned out to be more a place of safety than a refuge, but this was the type of refuge that was emerging at the time. It had one member of staff, a man who was the caretaker. It was derelict and housed five to eight women, as well as their children, in three dormitories. The kitchen was very dirty and there were not enough pots and pans to share. Everyone fought with everyone. It felt like only the poor women who were subjected to domestic violence, and in danger of homelessness, would find themselves there. The conditions were so bad that anyone with any money or any other alternative would be unlikely to go there or stay. The provisions were for poverty-stricken and/or desperate women.

The next morning, Naz went out to look for a job. She had stitches in her head and dry blood in her hair. She and the children walked up a steep hill towards a factory. She had heard that there were some Asian women working in the factory as seamstresses and that the factory belonged to an Asian man. The man told Naz that he could only employ her if she had permission from her husband. The reason for this was that he had previously given a job to an Asian woman, and when her husband had found out, he had come and beat him up. After that, he would only offer a job with the husband's consent. Naz could not imagine Yunis agreeing to this, and in any case, the police had told her not to go back to him. Naz walked back with the children to the refuge.

The next day she went to a trading estate where they had jobs packing boxes. Although they only needed people to pack boxes, they gave Naz a test to pass in order to have a job. She didn't pass the test. Some months later, she showed the same test to someone with a degree, and he could not do the test. Why they had that test she never knew. Naz also took a job in a small shop selling clothes, but there were no customers and she was bored, so she was sacked after one day.

The only job Naz was offered was modelling to promote new feather quilts which had just come into the market. She had to lie in a deep freezer in the supermarket with the quilt wrapped around her eight hours a day. She had to smile and look beautiful whilst lying in the freezer to show the shoppers that these new quilts could keep you warm, even in a deep freezer. She was offered £10 a day, which was good money those days. The job was not acceptable for all sorts of reasons, not least of which Naz hated being cold.

She went to the Community Relations office eventually and the head person, Chris, was a very kind man. He listened to Naz patiently, gave her travel expenses, and promised her that he would try to make some arrangements for her to stay safe. A few days later, Chris sent someone with a car to pick up Naz and the children from the refuge and bring them to the Community Relations office. Chris told Naz that there was a very decent English family who had put their name forward to accommodate refugees who were homeless, particularly Ugandan Asians. In 1973, a lot of these people were coming to England as refugees, due to Idi Amin's anti-colonial polices. The families of these Asians were originally from India, many of whom were transported to Africa during the British Raj to work for the British. When Idi Amin came into power in 1971, he threw them out of the country. Some went back to India, Pakistan and elsewhere, while others came to their 'motherland' Britain.

Chris told this English couple that although Naz and

her children were not from Uganda, they were in desperate need of shelter. He sent a driver to take Naz and the children to this couple's home, across the river in a middle-class area called Low Fell. It was a large detached double-fronted house, stone built with gardens all round. Naz could see that it was very clean, warm, and tastefully decorated and furnished. There were lots of books, newspapers and comics for the children. There was a music room with a piano and guitars and a big bay window looking down the valley, which was green and lush. The couple were in their fifties and introduced themselves as Alex and Pat. Alex was a famous songwriter and playwright, and had also been an English teacher, and Pat was also an English teacher. Naz could see they were warm and genuinely caring people. They made Naz and children very welcome and offered them hot drinks and cakes. Alex and Pat told Naz that they also had three children, two boys and an adopted daughter who was mixed race and "looked a bit look like your family." All three of their children were similar in age to Naz's children. Alex sent the driver from the community relations office to Yunis' address to pick up all their clothes and things and bring them back to their home.

Alex and Pat explained the situation to their children, Tom, Harry and Alice, when they came back from school, and like their parents, they were also friendly and relaxed. Naz's children were already used to living in an extended family, so they had no problems settling in. At first, Naz's children tried to talk to the other children in Punjabi, but when they didn't understand, they talked to them in Urdu and, when they still didn't understand, they started to speak in English. Rumi, the youngest, had the most difficulty in communicating in the beginning. She couldn't understand how other children did not understand the two languages she spoke. But she soon picked up English and started to communicate. That family didn't just share their house and food, they also shared their children's clothes. Pat was beautiful and very petite, so her clothes were not suitable for Naz, but Alex lent his jumpers, and outdoor jackets, and coats to her. Naz learned so much from that family. Alex and Pat were socialists and had books on socialism, Marxism and other left-wing writers. Naz read and learned about co-operative societies in the North of England, about industrialisation in Britain, about the miners' struggle, and about the fishery industry in South Shields. She learned about the biradari in agricultural society and the clans who look after each other and about modern industrial society when the state emerged to take some responsibility for people's welfare. And then, despite the welfare state, there were always charitable individuals like Alex and Pat who would look after people and come forward to help without wanting to be paid.

Alex and Pat were involved in politics and all sorts of political struggles. As Naz was already leaning towards the left, she thoroughly enjoyed reading their books and the Guardian newspaper every day. Alex and Pat would correct Naz's grammar and helped the children with their English language. They were also good cooks. Alex used to make bread and, in those days, lots and lots of bread. Pat would cook casseroles and pies, as well as Asian food. They all enjoyed the food and each other's company. Once, Pat ordered big sacks of chapatti flour and sacks of rice and dhal. When a Pakistani shopkeeper came to deliver the groceries, Alex was making the dough for bread whilst Naz was reading the newspaper and Pat was having a coffee. The shopkeeper went back to the Pakistani community and told everyone that he had gone to a very posh house across the river where an English man had two wives and six children, two white children, three brown and one mixed race. The most disturbing thing for him was why the man with two wives was making dough, while one wife was sitting reading the newspaper and the other was sitting enjoying coffee. This news was interesting for people in the Asian community and sensational – it spread like wildfire.

In the meantime, Yunis was putting lots of pressure on Naz's parents and making up abusive allegations, telling them to call her back to Pakistan. When Naz heard this, she was very upset and talked to Pat about it. Pat very kindly wrote a letter to Naz's parents and cleared up the situation, reassuring them that Naz and the children were safe with them.

Soon it was the Easter holidays. All the children were at home and Alex would take them swimming or to the parks or if the weather was good, he would take them to the sea. Sometimes, Alex would play his guitar and sing for the children. It was a very middle-class neighbourhood and most people were very kind, partly because they knew that Naz's family were guests of these very well-known people who lived in the nicest house on the road. Others were kind enough to help Naz and her children by inviting them for meals at their homes as well as giving things to Naz for when she would have her own home. There was a social worker living in the street and Naz overheard her telling someone that if Naz knew what kind of problems lay ahead, she would not be able to survive. This was partly true. There were all sorts of issues to think about, but Naz was not thinking about everything at once. She had heard the saying 'how to eat an elephant bit by bit,' so she dealt with issues day by day. For the present, she was very grateful to Alex and Pat for keeping them in their home. Pat went to the housing department with Naz, to help her put her name down on the housing list. Soon, Naz was offered a few flats in Newcastle. Pat encouraged Naz not to take the first accommodation offered but to wait until she was offered something suitable.

Pat also took Naz to see a solicitor, a young man called Jeremy Beecham, who became Lord Beecham. Mr Beecham was extremely patient and helpful. He sat with Naz and listened to her, and she could see that he had genuine empathy. He promised to do everything possible. Mr Beecham found and provided all the documents which Naz required to take Yunis to court to provide maintenance for her children. Pat accompanied Naz to the magistrate's court and Yunis was there with his girlfriend. This was the last time she saw Yunis.

In June 1973, after 3 months with Alex, Pat and family, Naz was offered a two bedroomed flat in Gateshead. She was over the moon to have her own place.

Chapter 9

Independence

Finally, Naz had her own place to live with her children. It was not perfect, but it was home and it was her home. The Tyneside flat was in a row of back-to-back terraced houses, each house having two flats. The two front doors were adjacent, one door opened to an upstairs flat and the other to the ground floor, their flat. The people from Pat and Alex's neighbourhood were very helpful. Andrew, a neighbour from their street, came with lots of paint and painted the entire flat with beautiful colours, making it look respectable. Other neighbours gave them second-hand furniture, bedding, pans, pots, and everything necessary to provide a home suitable for children. There was a coal fire in the living room, next to which was a small kitchen and then a bathroom which only had a bath. The toilet was outside. There were two bedrooms, Raza and Omer would share one bedroom, and Naz and Rumi the other. The boys were very happy to have a separate bedroom for themselves. The place started to look like a comfortable home quite quickly.

The flats on that side of the road belonged to Gateshead Council, and it was clear that they were council flats because all the doors were the same. The women from the council flats usually sat with their children on the front doorsteps. The flats on the opposite side of the road were also terraced, but were private flats that had recently been bought by the tenants. It was clear that they were private because they had a variety of fancy doors and windows. The families from those flats sat in their backyards rather than on their front doorsteps. The tension between the council tenants and the private owners was easy to see. The private flat owners did not want their children playing with the council flat children. To make matters worse, with Naz moving in, there was now an immigrant family in the street which brought down the council flat terrace's reputation even further! Naz was unaware of these differences and issues until much later. At the time, she was just very pleased to have a home.

The thought of the sole responsibility of the children and very little money was a bit daunting for Naz, but she had the confidence and believed that she would be able to manage. Naz could cook good food for little money, so the children had regular nourishing meals. She would cook in the kitchen and then they all sat in front of the fire in the evenings to have their meals. After the meal, they would talk about their life in Pakistan and talk in their mother tongue, Punjabi. The children never asked about Yunis or the events which had happened a few months earlier.

Nearby to the house, there was a very big park where

Naz would take the children regularly. The children played on the swings and slides while Naz enjoyed looking at the roses and other flowers. This reminded her of her childhood when they used to have big gardens in Resal Pur and she used to sleep in the flower beds. Afterwards, she would sit on the park bench with the children and talk to them. She used to tell them that everything would be very good in the future, and they would all be comfortable and happy. Somehow, she had this strong belief, difficult to explain to herself, that from then on, their future would get better.

The week after moving in, Naz enrolled Raza and Omer in the local school, a ten-minute walk from their home, and Rumi in a local nursery school. For herself, she enrolled to take O- and A-levels at Gateshead Technical College. The boys' school, Rumi's nursery, and the college were in three different directions from the house, but she would manage. Naz enrolled for three O- and two A-level GCEs, all of which she passed in one year. She had passed some equivalent exams in Pakistan but did not have the certificates with her, and in any case, even if she had, they wouldn't have been accepted. She did A-levels in Sociology and Psychology, which she particularly enjoyed and would be an indication of her future career.

Naz and the children spent the summer of 1973 adjusting to the new situation and the new environment, and preparing for the schools and college that they would attend in the autumn. They also got to know the nearby library. They borrowed and read books which they all loved to do, and found information about social events in the area. They would go there and enjoy discovering new things. There was also an art gallery nearby. Naz would take the children there to see paintings by various local and national artists. She could also borrow paintings and hang them in her flat for a limited time period.

Sometimes they went to the beach with a picnic, having to change two buses to get there. This reminded Naz of being in Pakistan when they all used to go for picnics as a family. The memory would make her sad but also happy that she was able to do this with her children. There were no Asian people living in the area and Naz felt somewhat conflicted about the children and herself being cut off from her own language and culture. She thought this was important for all of them. However, she felt it was necessary at that time for them to speak English and especially understand the Geordie accent. Although they were missing out on speaking their mother tongue, they kept some of the culture by eating a mixture of English and Pakistani food.

Whilst the family was settling into their new flat, the local vicar came to the door and introduced himself. Naz asked him in and offered him a cup of tea. The Vicar invited Naz to attend the church and said that the children could join the Sunday school. The vicar was totally unaware of the fact that Naz could have had a totally different religion or culture. Naz was chuckling inside, thinking how her ancestors would turn in their graves. Naz told the vicar that the children would go to Sunday school as it would be good for the children to do something on a Sunday. The children went to the Sunday school, where they made friends and enjoyed their time.

After quite a long time, Naz felt free of any external pressures and felt similar to what she had felt when she was younger. She wore what she wanted, and she was meeting new people. She was learning to be totally independent and to do her own thing. The sense of freedom and control of her own life was almost overwhelming. Raza and Omer were exploring new environments and working things out for themselves, but Rumi stayed closer to her mother and only went out with her. One day, Naz noticed the boys had some money. When Naz asked them the source of that money, they told her that they were returning empty pop bottles (receiving a few pence to return them) to Mr Thompson, who ran the corner shop. Raza and Omer were picking up the empty pop bottles from outside Mr Thompson's shop and returning his own bottles, which were stacked up outside his shop, waiting to be collected. The boys were unaware that the bottles belonged to him. Naz went to the shop and gave Mr Thompson his money back.

In the autumn, the children's school term and Naz's college classes started at the same time. The boys went together to their school, but Rumi went on her own, even though she was not yet five years old. Rumi's school was only a few streets away from home, but it was a lot for her to go to school on her own. It broke Naz's heart the first time she saw her little girl going to school alone. However, Rumi was brave and did not appear to be worried or nervous. She just got on with it. Naz was aware that her children were suffering by her being at college, especially Rumi. She was the first to get home from school, before the boys. When Naz got home, they would be standing outside on the doorstep in the cold and often Rumi would be cold and wet. Naz found it hard to manage all this. In Pakistan, children were never on their own and to see them standing outside hungry, cold and wet was heart-breaking. Yet, she was desperate to get out of poverty and to escape the evils and humiliation suffered by the poor everywhere in the world to greater or lesser degrees. Poverty comes with all sorts of difficulties, but Naz knew that the best way to get out of it was through education.

The teachers in the college insisted that everyone be in the class at 9am. If anyone was late, the teachers would get angry and blame them for disrupting the classroom. In those days, you could not use childcare as an excuse. No one made any allowances for parents with responsibilities. Most of the students were young and had no childcare responsibilities. Naz could see that the college had no room for flexibility or any awareness regarding the adult students. Therefore, Naz would not ask for any favours in case she upset the teachers in charge. She was very grateful to be able to have such a good education.

Upstairs from Naz and the children, there lived a woman who had a lot of male visitors, mostly in the evenings and mostly drunk. The male visitors would often get confused about the doors and sit in front of Naz's door. Though Naz and the children didn't go out in the evenings, it was still worrying to see the drunken men sitting at the front door. The woman upstairs was also upset about her visitors sitting at Naz's door because she thought Naz was in competition with her for the male visitors. She went to the Housing

Department and reported Naz saying too much noise was coming from the downstairs flat.

One day, when Naz came back from college, she let the children into the flat, made the fire and boiled the kettle to wash Rumi as they only had a cold-water tap. Just as Naz was about to start cooking, there was a knock on the door. When Naz opened the door, there was a woman in her fifties standing there. The woman introduced herself as the Housing Welfare Officer and her name was Barbara. Naz invited her in and listen to what Barbara had to say. Naz was very angry when she heard the false allegations made by the woman upstairs. She explained her everyday routine to Barbara and asked her how, with three children, she had the time to cause problems for anyone. Barbara heard Naz patiently and started to ask her personal questions about her family, education, and circumstances. Naz was cooking whilst talking and asked Barbara if she would like to eat with them since Naz's family tradition was always to invite visitors to eat with the family. Barbara was delighted and had a meal with Naz and the children. While Naz was clearing and washing the dishes, Barbara read a story to the children and put them to bed. After that, Barbara asked Naz if she went out much. Naz said she couldn't go out because of the children and college work. Barbara offered to babysit in the evenings and weekends so that Naz could go out if she wanted to. That day, Barbara left the flat quite late and when she opened the door, she stumbled upon a drunken man sitting and leaning on Naz's door. Barbara said she thought Naz should not be living there, as it wasn't a suitable place for a family, and she left.

Barbara became a friend for life, and she was always there for Naz whenever she needed help, including letting the children in from school. It was good for the children to come back from their schools and not have to stand outside in the cold. And it was good for Naz to have a break from rushing back from college. As an older person, Barbara was very good for the children. At Christmas, Naz bought a Christmas tree and some toys for the children. The college had a smart Christmas party in Newcastle Guildhall, and Barbara babysat so that Naz could attend. The only dressy thing Naz had to wear was a sari, but as the weather was so cold, she put on 'long johns' underneath it. Naz met lots of people at the party, which had a relaxed atmosphere and was fantastic. It was Naz's first party in England.

1973 was coming to an end, and it had been an eventful year, to say the least. So much had happened from leaving Rawalpindi and then being on a roller coaster, never having time to think or make plans for the future. Naz was moving with the events and making the most of the situation, but she was very concerned that the children might be suffering. They had witnessed so much violence by their father, and then moved from one place to another. Everything had been unfamiliar for them, from learning a new language, being in new schools and adjusting to new situations all the time. Naz thought that the worst part was that the children had watched their mother being abused. Naz herself had never experienced this sort of violence; her own father had always been very respectful to her mother. They laughed and joked all the time. One thing Naz promised herself was that she would never let this happen again and her children would never witness this kind of situation again. Naz may not have realised this at the time, but she had a lot of pent-up anger. She was angry with herself for being in this situation and she was desperate to get out of all the mess and instability. The anger gave her energy and drive to move on. She was also determined not to depend on anyone, and this stopped her from opening up to many people. Although she made friends and engaged with new people, it was difficult for her to share her personal life and feelings at that time.

There were people like Chris from the Community Relations Office, Pat and Alex, Lord Beecham, and now Barbara and a few other friends. Naz realised that she was incredibly lucky to have met these amazing people who had held her hand at her most difficult times. Naz accepted the fact that it was rare for people to escape situations like she had been in, unless there were people to help. They encouraged her and enabled her to stand on her own two feet in order to move forward. Naz thought that these people who believed in her, had perhaps recognised her inner strength that she had as a result of her loving upbringing.

It was in her 'nasseb' to come across the most helpful and empathetic people, the people who would guide her along the right path every step of the way. It is true that no one ever reaches their destiny, or finds success, without the help of good people who offer their hand of good will and confidence along the way.

Naz began to realise that had she may not have had the same opportunities had she been more connected to the Asian community. At that time in the 1970s, many from both the Asian and English communities thought that after having three children, Naz's life should only be about bringing up the children. And that she should have gone back to her own family for safety and protection. But Naz had her own aspirations and ambitions. She had tasted a 'good life' earlier when she was in Pakistan, and she knew what was possible and would at least hope and wish for it.

Sometime later, Naz reflected that if she had had her own family around her in Britain, it would have been a comfort and may have made it easier to settle in. However, on the other hand, she would also have been constrained due to cultural expectations. If Naz's family had been around, Yunis would not have dared to be so violent, but it is also likely that she would also have been persuaded to stay in the relationship for one reason or another. Naz would have been trapped in a very unhappy marriage and would never have been able to fulfil her own potential.

Naz felt similarly about living within the Asian community. She and her children would have enjoyed the language and culture, but she would have missed out on some amazing people she had met in her life. The women in the first immigrant community did not mix with British culture much, and often relied on their husbands and children to connect with the wider community. This was partly due to the language barrier, and the lack of opportunities to practise the language, and partly due to family constraints. In Tyneside at that time, the Asian community lived in the same area and most of the families were from a particular area of Pakistan.

This community was a homogeneous community and Naz would not have fitted in for all sorts of reasons. Instead, Naz found herself feeling free and liberated in the true meaning of the word and embraced British culture with open arms. She enjoyed the language, politics, and values, as well as the community and culture. In some ways, she thought that this was probably what her parents had really wanted for her. Her father had especially wanted her to have the freedom to be happy, but her mother, with her own strong character, had likely also wanted this for Naz. Even if they had not been aware of it themselves, her parents were liberal people, constrained in their culture, yet radical in their activities.

In the summer of 1974, the college and schools closed for the summer. Naz and the children had survived and come out stronger. Barbara saw Naz and the children regularly and one day, she came with a set of keys in her hand and offered Naz a house in a very nice estate in Gateshead – a three-bedroomed house in a street called Appian Place.

Barbara helped Naz and the children to move into their new home and they said goodbye to the old flat.

Chapter 10

Appian Place

Appian Place was a tree-lined street, and the house was just beautiful. It had a garden in the front and the back, with an apple tree. It was a small, semi-detached three-bedroom house with a nice kitchen, a downstairs bathroom, and the living room had a bay window. There was central heating and hot water taps. Absolute heaven! The boys had one bedroom, Rumi had another, and Naz had a bedroom to herself for the first time ever. The thing Naz most liked was that it was light and bright. It was a very respectable working-class neighbourhood where all the houses were owned by Gateshead Council. There were very nice neighbours and a parade of shops nearby and their lives became much more pleasant. People took a lot of pride in their homes and gardens. The mature, tree-lined streets in the area looked and felt like a very settled community. When Naz and her family moved in, no one in the community thought that Naz and her family were strange or different. It was a refreshing change for her.

On the other side of the semi-detached house was a middle-aged couple, Beth and John Waters, who had a grown-up son who went to work, and a very young daughter who went to school with Rumi. There was an unusually large gap in age between the son David and the daughter Alice, but no one talked about it. Being next door, Naz quickly learned about the everyday routine of the Waters family. Every morning Beth would make sandwiches for her husband and son, who took the same bus to go to work each day, and came back each day at the same time. Beth would have their tea ready and then they would all watch the TV. On Saturdays, John and David watched the football, of course, because they were Newcastle supporters, and then had their tea. Every Sunday morning, John would take a cup of tea to Beth in bed and then put the meat in the oven, peel the potatoes and go to the pub with David, where they watched football with their friends. Beth would have the Sunday lunch ready by the time they came back, their main meal in the middle of the day. After Sunday lunch, John and David would snooze on the sofa in front of the TV. Sometimes, when Newcastle football team lost, Naz's family would hear voices from next door, perhaps arguing about the 'footy.' Beth would bake all Sunday afternoon to have food for tea and the rest of the week, and Naz would enjoy the beautiful aromas of baking each Sunday.

On the right side of the house, there was a small lane that everyone called 'the cut' which cut through to the main road. It was mostly children who went to school that way. On the other side of the lane, lived the Nelson family. Mrs

Nelson was a widow and had three beautiful daughters. One was sixteen and called Cilla, and the other two, Jenifer and Jane, were Raza and Omer's age. They were all blond with long hair and all had the most beautiful blue eyes. The family was isolated in the community because Mrs Nelson was German. Mr Nelson had fallen in love with this German woman, and they had married and had three children, but unfortunately, he died later. The community ostracised the Nelson family because of their German origin. Mrs Nelson was very shy, and she herself did not make much effort to mix. She may have made efforts when the family first moved into the area, but by the time Naz arrived, she preferred not to mix. Naz and her family fell in love with the girls and the Nelson family took to them like a 'duck to water.' The girls were always around playing with the children, eating with them, and Cilia, the oldest, would babysit for Naz.

Naz enrolled the children into new schools for the autumn term. Luckily, there were lots of children in the neighbourhood who went to the same schools, so the children had no problems getting there and Naz felt less anguish because Rumi did not have to go to school on her own. It was nice for Naz to see that her children went together with other children in the area.

Naz applied to Newcastle Polytechnic (now Northumbria University) to study social work, which was a three-year course. Naz was interviewed by the head of the Department, Miss Irene Foster, who turned down her application saying she did not have enough social work experience. Naz sat outside Miss Foster's office all day until she finished interviewing all the candidates and then went into her office. Naz simply refused to leave the college until she was given a place on the course. She argued with Miss Foster for hours, finally convincing her that she had enough life experience to go on the social work course.

Gateshead Education Authority awarded Naz a very handsome educational grant and travel expenses. That, plus child benefit, was enough money to buy food and the children's uniforms, but there was no money left for anything else. Naz had one pair of jeans that she wore for three years. In the end, the jeans were so worn out and ragged at the bottom of the legs that on her practice placement, people would make fun of her and call her Naz with raggy pants. Much later, it became fashionable to wear raggy jeans like hers.

Naz enjoyed the course but argued throughout about Western ethnocentric values being taught as universal values. She enjoyed arguing and discussing with students and teachers alike, especially about 'care', whether it was to do with childcare, adult care, or community care. As Naz was the first and the only Asian person on the course, there were lots of challenges in relation to various theories and social work practice. Some teachers and students engaged with these discussions and found it refreshing and thought provoking. Others just ignored them, which Naz didn't mind. Overall, the social work course was much more enjoyable than Naz's previous college experience and the staff were relaxed about attendance and deadlines.

In the summer holidays, Naz worked in local old people's

residential homes, partly for the experience but mostly for the income. There she was just a student, working on her career. Naz was horrified to see the practice and attitudes of the staff. The residents' lives had to fit the institution, rather than the institution being there to facilitate life for the residents. There must be some order in an institution, but to be so regimented at the expense of the residents was not acceptable. They had to get out of bed at the crack of dawn and go to bed very early in the evening at the convenience of the staff. If a resident could not get out of bed, there would be no breakfast for the person. Apart from the practical side, the attitudes of the staff were very patronising to elderly people. The matron would talk to them as if they were children, and Naz found it humiliating. There were no concerns for residents' dignity and respect. No one knocked on the door to enter someone's room. Male staff were bathing women and female staff were bathing men. It seemed that people who were old were not regarded as a person in their own right. Naz used to listen to their stories. Some had been teachers when they were young and others had worked for the Council – people with responsible jobs. Naz would think of her own grandparents and remembered when she used to help her grandmother and great grandmother, washing and oiling their long hair and platting it to look nice and tidy. She also remembered that after helping them to bathe, she would rub talcum powder on their bodies to keep them dry and to smell nice. Naz got very angry with the staff 'warehousing' the elderly in this residential home.

There were very few hot days in the North during the

summer, so whenever there was good weather, Naz would take the residents into the garden. This gave them a break from sitting in heated rooms with their jumpers on. She also tried to play games with them in the garden. The staff would get angry with Naz and tell her off. They saw her care as a waste of time and thought it brought chaos to the home, which was unacceptable to the Matron and the other staff. The Matron and the staff thought that, because Naz was Asian, she did not understand the culture and therefore was having difficulties fitting in. For her part, Naz thought that the elders in society should be valued and respected and not be treated like this. The tension between the staff and Naz got serious. Naz thought this was bad practice and not the way to treat elders and the Matron did not want this young student/carer to raise questions. In the end, Naz went to see the director of residential homes and reported her experiences. There was a full inquiry and later the home was closed. The residents were moved into a nearby home, which was much better. The reports went to Miss Foster at the college. Naz explained to her that her own background and experiences helped her enrich social work practice and add value. Miss Foster was happy with this explanation.

By this time, the children had totally forgotten how to speak Urdu and Punjabi. Naz was acutely aware that her children were moving away from her own culture. As she herself enjoyed speaking several languages and had a good understanding of other cultures, she wanted the same for the children. But this did not seem possible. There wasn't a place where they could go and practice their mother tongue and learn about the culture. The only place was a mosque miles away from home. Also, Naz had heard about the reputation of some mosques where the teachers gave corporal punishment, so Naz was not going to send her children to such places. However, the children were interested in European languages and culture, which made Naz happy, and she encouraged her children to learn these new languages.

Soon, Naz had another social work placement, this time in Sunderland Hospital. This time, her supervisor was a competent and experienced person, and she learned a lot. She saw a lot of poverty and deprivation in Sunderland. She visited different homes and would often face mistrust and lack of confidence from the families. Partly it was due to her being a student and partly because she was an Asian social worker. Some people might never have met an Asian person, never mind a social worker. This was a very difficult placement for Naz, for various reasons. She was finding it hard to cope with some social work practice and the boundaries between professional and private lives. The professional ethic of not disclosing anything about your own life was alien to Naz because her background and culture had taught her to be open. She felt that the profession of social work in the British class system was middle-class, but she herself felt working class because she had been very poor since coming to Britain. She also struggled in college when she raised issues of race and class with teachers and fellow students. These were issues that they didn't seem to have thought about before. This caused a lot of stress and soul searching for everyone. Sometimes, Naz experienced self-doubt and a crisis of confidence, and she thought that perhaps she was not articulate enough to express her point of view. But at other times, she felt frustrated that some people were not willing to think 'outside the box.' Generally, she felt under a lot of pressure, not just on the placement but also with college work and managing a home.

As the summer term was ending in 1977, two new staff joined the social work department in the college. One of them was the Head of the Department who was a beautiful young woman from the South. She was highly intelligent and highly competent and looked very relaxed. Her hair was stylish, with a 'just got out of bed' style. The students immediately fell in love with her. The other new member of staff was a young man called Malcolm who was a criminologist and a most unusually dressed young man. He wore cotton dungarees, one arm and leg black and one arm and leg white, with a toothbrush stuck in his front pocket. Naz liked his radical style, and he turned out to be a brilliant teacher.

As the classes and assessments came to an end, everyone was exhausted and drained, particularly Naz. Malcolm suggested that some of the students and staff go to the Edinburgh Festival to see a play by Jimmy Boyle, the Scottish Glaswegian former gangster. Naz jumped at the chance as she thought about all her memories of that city, her Glasgow connections, and her time in Scotland where her two sons were born. Naz went for the day with her friends and some of the staff, the first time she had been to Edinburgh. The route from Newcastle to Edinburgh along the coast road was magical, with the heather-topped hills all in different colours and lots of sheep and cattle. It was the most relaxing journey

Naz had ever been on. At the border, there was a single man in his kilt playing the bagpipes. Naz thought about her grandfather in the Scottish Artillery Regiment in India and on the Afghanistan border. On the route, there were quaint little tea shops and Naz and her friends stopped for a cup of tea at one of them. Naz had made parathas for everyone to have for breakfast with tea en route, and everyone was happy.

Edinburgh was beautiful. Naz loved the shops, the restaurants and the hum of Princes Street. It looked very cosmopolitan with people who looked affluent, judging by their clothes and footwear. The festival was full of people from all over Britain and the world. The Edinburgh Festival was a truly international event. There were a variety of plays and musical events and they spotted lots of well-known people who were there to enjoy themselves. There were a lot of beautiful art and craft shops and food stalls with international cuisines. Naz went into a smart women's clothes shop where she saw a burnt red colour velvet jumpsuit which she tried on and loved. She used her credit card to buy it, and blew her money, which she had never done before. Naz told herself that this money was an investment, as the suit would be for an interview for a job.

The play by Jimmy Boyle was a heartfelt emotional drama which pulled at the heart strings. The story, the acting and the atmosphere were electric. Naz had never seen anything like it before. She felt happy and relieved to be away from the stress of the course work and she enjoyed being with her friends. This was a lovely time for her. She felt very optimistic about the future and confident that from now on, things were going her way. In June, before she had the results from college, Naz applied for a job as a social worker in the West End of Newcastle. She was offered an interview on 4th July 1977. She put on her burnt red jumpsuit, which made her very happy and confident. She gave a good interview and was offered a job subject to passing her course, which she did. Later that month, Naz was invited through her connections to meet Mohammed Ali, the boxer in South Shields. When she got the invitation, she thought she had died and gone to heaven. It was not a one-to-one meeting with him by any means. There were lots of people there but she got to meet him and shake hands. That was one of her very best days.

Naz was looking forward to her new job and felt confident that she would be able to make a difference to people's lives, particularly women's lives. She could not believe that she would return as a qualified social worker to the area that she had left as a battered wife four years ago.

The family in 1952. Naz sits behind her uncle Tariq.

The family in Rawalpindi in 1966. Raza sits on her grandfather's lap and Omer with on one of Naz's brothers at the back.

Naz with her children in Rawalpindi.

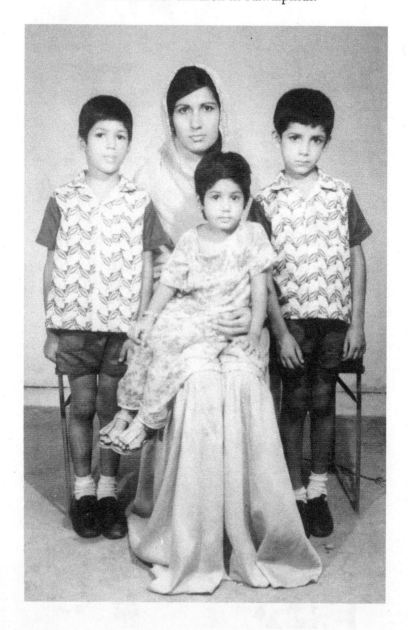

Freedom and peace; walking in the Himalayas, 1980.

In the Snow, 1974.

The children going to Sunday school in Gateshead, 1975.

Naz at the Edinburgh festival in 1977.

The children with their dog, Henry, in Appian Place.

Independence, 1974.

Chapter 11

Cruddas Park

The summer of 1977 was good in every way for Naz and her family. She had a job and a second-hand car, and travelled from Gateshead to Newcastle to her office, which was only about a twenty-minute drive. Having a car, Naz and the children could explore Northumberland's beautiful countryside and the coast, where they would have picnics and play games. Their favourite place was Rothbury, where the children would paddle in the river, and they went there again and again. They would also go to Alnwick by the sea and have fish and chips. Their neighbours, the Nelson girls, would also go with Naz and the children.

The summer was warm, and Naz went to a Laura Ashley shop and bought herself two dresses, one blue with little flowers, the other with red flowers. They were her favourite colours. The dresses, called tent dresses, were loose and long down to her shins. She also bought herself 'Jesus' sandals and wearing the dresses and sandals, she thought she now looked like a 'proper' social worker.

The social work office was in a building which had been a bank some time ago, but had to be shut down for security reasons. Most office rooms were dark because they had no windows and no natural light. Only the reception area on the ground floor had windows. It was an Area Office at the west end of Newcastle and was called Cruddas Park. The name was very deceptive, since the area was like a concrete jungle with hardly any greenery, trees, or parkland. It had very dense housing with back-to-back built terraced houses but mostly Tyneside type flats. Some had backyards, but not all the houses or flats had outside spaces.

Most of the population in that area was unemployed and receiving benefits. It was a very mixed community, and the majority were Asian who spoke Punjabi and Bengali and a few who spoke Urdu. There was an Irish community and also a large English working-class area. Some estates were so dangerous that social workers hesitated to visit, even during the day. There was a mosque and an Asian grocery shop in the area, and a few small corner shops that sold cigarettes and alcohol. The area was crawling with vicious looking dogs and moneylenders who were either lending or collecting money like vultures.

A week into her job, Naz was called to Mr Read, who was the Director of Social Services in the Head Office. She was terrified and wondered why she was being called to the Director's office so early into her new job. She asked her area manager, but he did not know the reason either. Naz went to the head office at the arranged time. This was her first time at the Head Office and the first time she had met the Director of Social Services. He was a pleasant man and he could see that Naz was stressed. He told her that she had nothing to be worried about. Apparently, some Asian Community leaders and the Community Relations Officer, who was also an Asian man, told the Director that he had made a terrible mistake by employing Naz as a social worker. He had told Mr Read that Naz would lead all the women in the community astray, particularly the Asian women, and that it would cause unrest in the community. The Director went on to say that the only reason he was telling Naz this was because he wanted to warn her to be careful and question who her friends in the city were. By that time, Naz was so stressed that tears started pouring from her eyes, but she quickly then managed to compose herself. She told Mr Read her story, and what a tough journey it had been to become a social worker and to get to this stage. She told him how she wanted to do the best for her clients, what she felt was right. She was employed to work with women and children, and that's what she was going to do. The Director nodded in agreement and Naz said goodbye and left his office.

Naz's first social work visit was to a general hospital where an Indian lady was admitted for physical ill health, but there was also suspicion about problems of mental health. This happened to be the same hospital where Naz had been admitted after she was beaten up by her husband. That morning, Naz had put on her traditional dress, the shalwar kamiz, because she thought that the client who was ill and possibly confused would feel more comfortable speaking to someone who looked familiar. Naz arrived on the ward, where this woman was the only Asian patient. She was in her mid-twenties. Her long hair was untidy, and she looked very neglected. Naz held her hand and greeted her in her own language, and the client immediately relaxed and smiled. Naz could see the client was heavily medicated as her face was blemished and she looked confused. Naz and the client were talking, very relaxed and sometimes laughing, when a male nurse walked into the ward and said that she could not talk in her own language. Naz was not sure whether the nurse was aware that Naz was a social worker. She became very angry and stood up and said to the nurse, "Show me where it is written that people cannot talk in their own language and who are you to say this to a patient?"

Naz very quickly realised that her anger was disproportionate and was coming from her own experience. She calmed down and admitted to herself that it was the memory of that hospital that was making her so angry. Nevertheless, the male nurse was wrong to try to stop them from speaking in their own language.

Naz was the first Asian worker in the city, so she had no role models, but she was determined to work in her own way. From then on, Naz had to think very carefully about her reactions. She continued to be enthusiastic, compassionate and empathetic but she also realised that she couldn't let her own past traumas colour her judgement. On the other hand, she also realised that she should use her personality and her life experiences, her language skills, and her cultural background to support her clients in a positive way. For example, at that time there was a wave of children being taken into care and Naz sometimes heard social workers associate success with the number of children he or she had taken into care. As Naz herself had come from a big family network, she worked hard to keep children in the community with their families. Particularly in Asian families. She explored the family networks as well as their extended families to find support for the children. She worked similarly with the Irish and English working-class communities. Rather than looking at the issues as an individual family problem, she saw these problems as community issues. When Naz did take risks in not taking children into care but supporting families instead, this sometimes made her seniors very nervous.

Naz learned later in her career that this was good social work practice which social workers, trained as child care officers, were doing at that time in other areas of the country. Apart from issues of poverty, there were the issues that related to poverty such as unemployment, relationship problems, parenting skills, ill health, mental health, housing issues, lack of education, legal disputes and immigration. To deal with these issues, Naz was involved in setting up services for her clients, alongside other professionals, service from organisations such as the Family Service Unit, Law Centre, Credit Union, Tenants Association, Women's Refuge, Neighbourhood Centres as well as Adult Education.

It was a very interesting area to work in and through her work, she met a variety of people. The Lord Mayor lived in one of the flats on a council estate. His limousine could be seen in front of his flat, which had two large lamps on either side of it, just to show that the Lord Mayor lived there. The children from the estate would climb onto the limousine and no one would tell them off. The mayor himself was a very nice person and very available to the public. Naz also worked with Mr Jeremy Beecham (later Lord Beecham) who was once her solicitor and became Leader of the Newcastle Upon Tyne City Council. Naz thoroughly enjoyed her work, particularly working with women. Some Asian women were quite critical of her dress sense and thought that she should not be wearing Laura Ashley dresses, but her Shalwar Kamiz instead. They believed this would be more respectable. In response, Naz used to laugh and say okay, next time.

Naz saw a lot of poverty in the West End of Newcastle. She saw very small babies wrapped in newspapers, people living in derelict houses, no food in the house, and children involved in petty theft. All of this was having a big impact on her own health in terms of burnout and exhaustion. In those days, women were afraid to mention their childcare responsibilities as they thought their employers might think they were not fully concentrating on their work, or that it might stop them being promoted. Like other women, Naz would not take time out from work, and she worked harder than others to prove that her childcare responsibilities did not affect her social work duties.

Every day after finishing work, Naz would go to the Asian shop which was very close to her office and buy fresh meat, vegetables, fruits, and spices. The shop was the only big Pakistani grocery and meat shop in Newcastle at the time. Naz found the shop very friendly, and the aroma of the spices, fruit and vegetables was very familiar. The shop was run by several brothers. A couple of them would work on the meat counter, the other two would be on the till and then a few of them would do the wholesale shopping and deliveries to the restaurants. In those days, when you bought a chicken, it was alive. You would hear a big noise from the back of the shop of someone running alongside the chicken, rushing like mad and then an eerie quiet. Then you would know your chicken had been caught and killed. They would bring the chicken into the shop, still half bleeding, and they would ask you whether you wanted, "Skin off and pieces?" You would nod and within minutes, the chicken would be in your bag, still warm.

Naz never saw any of their women in the shop, except their elderly mother, who would be sitting on the chair by the till and talking to the customers. Naz liked the old lady and she would always stop for Gup Shap, chit chat. The old lady would always comment on Naz's clothes and say things like, "Now you are earning money, you must be able to afford a decent Shalwar Kamiz," not knowing how much the Laura Ashely dress cost. Naz used to laugh and think it was so nice that Asian elderly still feel they can pass that sort of comment without being afraid of the reaction. Naz picked up a lot of gossip about the community from the shop; sometimes it was useful but usually it was a waste of time.

Naz would go home and cook a big meal and the family would eat together. Then the children would wash the dishes and clear the kitchen. The boys were not doing very well in secondary school. Children from other areas joined the school and the tensions amongst the children from different areas increased every day. Naz tried to gather people from the neighbourhood to put pressure on the school to stop the feuding among the children, but no one took much interest. Raza and Omer came out worst as they were the only non-white children in the school. One morning before school, Naz saw Raza and Omer stuffing rolled-up newspapers and heavy books into their bags. She found out that they were preparing for a fight in the school. Naz thought about when her youngest child Rumi would go to that school, and she did not want her to get involved in gang warfare. That was the last straw and Naz decided to move into a catchment area where she heard that schools were better.

Naz saw a house in Low Fell, a middle-class area with better schools. It was a beautiful Victorian house which had been boarded up. The house looked as though it had been sleeping for a long time. It was a stone-built house, double fronted and facing south. It was September and beautiful climbers covered the walls in autumn colours of vivid red and sharp yellow. There were gardens to the front and side, and the back of the house was attached to the end of a terrace of houses. The house stretched between two roads and on the front gate was written 'The Gables.' Without looking inside, Naz fell in love with the house and she went straight away to the Estate Agent. The Estate Agent told her that it would be a secret bid and whoever bid the highest would be able to purchase the house. Apparently, Naz's bid was the lowest and someone else, a very rich person, bought it for his daughter. Naz could not sleep for many nights because she was not able to afford 'The Gables.'

She was so heartbroken that she did not bother to look for another house. A few months later, The Gables was back on the market and Naz got excited again. She put in an offer of exactly the same amount she had offered in the first place, and it was accepted.

Naz went to the building society for a mortgage where she met a Mr Hudson who was slightly built with a kind face. Naz gave him all her details and Mr Hudson's face lit up when he heard Naz was a social worker. Naz had always thought that her face was a big give away; as soon as people saw her, they wanted to tell her their problems or maybe she encouraged people to pour them out. And it happened again here. Mr Hudson told her that he thought she would understand what he was going to say. Naz reassured him that she would listen to him, and if she could help, she would. Mr Hudson told Naz that he was married and had children. Naz thought that he might say something like, 'My wife doesn't understand me,' which she had heard many times before. He did indeed say this, but the problem was not what Naz expected. As a social worker, she had learned to expect anything, but this took her by surprise. He told Naz that every day after work he went to a place where everyone dressed in women's clothes. He said that afterwards, he always changed back into his work clothes and went home. Naz listened to him very carefully and told him that in Pakistan there were lots of people who were openly cross dressers, so she was familiar with this issue. In fact, in Pakistan, there is not much difference in women's and men's everyday clothes anyway, sometimes just a bit of difference in colours; traditional clothing for women is the shalwar kamiz, with trouser type bottoms. Naz always wondered why, when women wore men's clothes, like suits or trousers, no one minded, but when men wore women's clothes, it was not found acceptable. She wondered if it might be a form of sexism that originated in an earlier period of history.

Naz told Mr Hudson that when she moved into The Gables, she was going to have a big party and he would be invited. He could come whatever way he chose to dress. Later, Naz did have a party in The Gables and Mr Hudson did come. He got changed at her house and she offered him her sparkling sari, which he loved but refused. There were a lot of social workers at the party, and he had a very good time.

In November 1980, Naz finished work and went as usual to the Pakistani shop to pick up some groceries. She saw a notice written in Urdu announcing that Yunis had died and his funeral was later that evening. In the Muslim religion, the deceased are buried as soon as possible. Naz went home and told her children. Rumi was too young to understand, as she had had the shortest relationship with him. However, Omer got very angry and said, "why are we talking about it? I may as well pick up the Evening Chronical and go to a stranger's funeral." Naz could understand Omer's anger, but she herself was not feeling anything, not even anger. Raza said to Naz, "Mum, if you want to go, I will go with you," so Naz put on her white sari and Raza got dressed in funeral clothes and they left. Naz was now technically a widow because she had never had a divorce from Yunis, nor had he ever paid any maintenance. But Naz had never thought of herself as married, so she did not think of herself as a widow either. By the time Naz and Raza went to his house, his body had been flown to Pakistan, so Naz and Raza never saw him.

Later, Naz's family in Pakistan found out about the death of Yunis, but they were oblivious to Naz's situation. When they had a proper death announcement, her mother was crying and wailing that her daughter had become a widow at such a young age. People were visiting Naz's parents' house to pay their condolences and feeling sorry for the children and Naz. In England, Naz was thinking 'Thank God' she had left him when she had, or otherwise, she would still be an uneducated and 'battered' widow.

Chapter 12

The Gables

The Gables was built in 1900 and the last owner was a lady who had been born in the previous century and who had died in the late 1960s. No one had lived there after that. Joseph Swan, one of the earlier inventors of the light bulb, had also lived in a nearby house. The Gables was one of the houses that had early electricity and it also still had the remnants of gas lights. Later, Naz found out the reason why the house was so cheap. It was because the main beam of the house was held up by a car jack. Naz was not too concerned because she thought that if the house had been standing for so long with the car jack, it would continue to stand for much longer.

The Gables was a very big house with two very large bedrooms and one small one, and a very large bathroom upstairs. Downstairs, there were two large reception rooms, both with bay windows and a very big kitchen and breakfast room. There was also a garage and a workshop and a drive at the back for a car. Naz went to an auction and picked up second-hand sofas, a dining table, chairs and some carpets. It all looked very nice in the old house.

However, the house was large with long corridors which took up lots of space and made the house very cold. The windows and doors were all drafty, which made it very expensive to run. All in all, the house was not practical, but Naz thought it was beautiful. To increase her income, Naz had lodgers in one of the front rooms until she could afford to run the house herself.

The children started to go to better schools, and they seemed to be much happier. They made friends for life in this area. In the morning, children would gather in Naz's house and then they would all walk up the hill with Raza and Omer. Rumi would walk in the other direction, which was not too far, and meet her friends at the school gate. Raza and Omer's friends also loved the house. They would run along the corridors laughing, screaming, and shouting. It was just as well that there were no neighbours close by to be annoyed. When Naz was at work, children in the area would come to The Gables and enjoy playing, eating and drinking and spending a lot of their time there, sometimes much to the annoyance of their parents. The children loved the Bohemian and relaxed lifestyle of Naz and her children. Lots of food and cooking went on there and it was okay for everyone to join in. As the house was close to the main road, people often popped in for a cup of tea or curry. Some children are still family friends and a couple of them regard Naz as their second mother.

When Raza and Omer, particularly Omer, were getting older, they would have parties at home and go out to parties. All their friends would gather at The Gables and start getting ready from 5 o'clock onward. Abba and Barbra Streisand songs would be playing as loudly as possible – you could hear 'Dancing Queen' for miles. The house would be full of boys and the bathroom would be occupied for hours. They would use Naz's makeup, clothes, jewellery, and anything they could get their hands on. The house would look like a battlefield after they left. Raza had a girlfriend, so he would spend a lot of time at his girlfriend's house as he got on well with her parents. They acted like a serious couple.

Rumi would mostly be out riding her bike. She enjoyed being on her bike like Naz did when she was her age, and she also spent a lot of time visiting her school friends. Her friends were quieter, either quietly playing or talking in one room or giggling or talking in a corner. The Gables was definitely a party house and Naz and the children never missed an opportunity to have a party, though it was mostly Omer and Naz who had them. Raza and Rumi had different interests. There were always visitors staying, people from other parts of the country as well as other parts of the world. Once, one of Naz's cousins came from Pakistan to visit her. While he was trying to find her house, he saw The Gables and was convinced this had to be Naz's house because, he thought, 'only Naz could live in a house like this.'

Later, Naz bought some hens and kept them in the garden, and they would have fresh eggs. Passers-by would bring their children to show them the hens. Naz was happy that people in the community brought their children to see them so the children could see where eggs come from. But soon, when Naz's children went to feed the hens, they began noticing that one or two hens were missing. The children were very upset about this. One day, they told Naz that Henry Ator, their favourite hen, was missing and the thought of Henry Ator lying on someone's Sunday dinner table was unbearable. Therefore, they decided to get rid of all the hens.

Sometime later, when Naz's parents heard about Yunis' death and that Naz and Yunis had separated, and that Naz had been living on her own with the children, they become very concerned. When Naz saw that her parents were very worried about the children, she decided to invite them over for a few weeks so that they could see for themselves that all was well. Shahjahan and Mumtaz agreed to come over for a few weeks in 1982. Naz set up a comfortable bedroom for them in the dining room, where she made sure that they had a comfortable bed and everything they needed. By that time, the lodgers had gone and only the children's friends, who usually popped in before and after school, came to the house.

Naz picked her parents up from Heathrow Airport and brought them home to Gateshead. They loved the house and were very pleased to see their grandchildren. They also liked Gateshead and Newcastle and loved seeing so much greenery, lots of parks and lots of flowers. They thought Northumberland was beautiful and that the coast and the castles were stunning. They were a bit surprised that they didn't see any children playing on the streets. They missed not seeing very young children around, apart from the ones who were their grandchildren's friends.

Shahjahan, who had once been a sportsman, loved to go for long walks. Once, he was walking on the Tyne Bridge, and was surprised that the bridge was a similar design to Sydney Harbour Bridge in Australia, which he had also walked on when he had visited Sydney in the 1950s. Later, he was told that the design of the Tyne Bridge had been a basis for Sydney Harbour Bridge. Shahjahan was still very tall and handsome, and he was wearing his very elegant Shalwar Kamiz and his Royal Airforce sunglasses while he was walking up and down the Tyne Bridge, looking at the bridge with great interest. There were some engineers working on the bridge and when they saw Shahjahan paying so much attention to the bridge, they thought he was some rich Arab wanting to buy it, like London Bridge which was bought by Americans. One of the engineers said to Shahjahan 'would you like to buy this bridge sir' and Shahjahan replied, 'of course if you can deliver it to my home in Pakistan.' Then they all had a good laugh. Thankfully, it was the 1980s and not the time of writing this or he might have been arrested as a terrorist, paying the amount of attention as he was to the bridge.

One of the things that racist people do is to dehumanise black and Asian people, and make them other, different, separate, not like 'us'. They have a 'them' vs 'us' mentality. When Naz was working in Cruddas Park, some of her colleagues would say 'Oh, you must have come on the banana boat' or pass remarks which were overtly racist as well as sexist. In those days, people got away with it, especially when they were in a position of power. One day, Naz's father turned up in her office in Cruddas Park and when her colleagues saw this very elegant, tall man in a suit, they asked her if this was really her father because they were surprised by his appearance. It seemed that just because Naz was an immigrant, people assumed her father would be a shop keeper or a bus driver, which was the image that many white people had if you were an immigrant.

After Yunis died, and even before Naz left his home, she had never had time to think about him, nor did she want to think about him. But when Naz's parents came over, they wanted to meet Yunis' partner Ruby. Naz understood why her parents wanted to meet her. They just wanted to find out more about Yunis and the reasons why he had behaved so badly to their daughter. Naz understood that her parents wanted to know more about the man they chose for their daughter and to bring some closure to the saga of her marital life. Naz was finding all this very awkward because the last time she had seen Ruby was ten years ago when Naz returned from Pakistan and Ruby was standing in the shop with Yunis. However, she took her parents to see Ruby at her house. Ruby lived with her children from her first partner in a small flat on a large council estate. She looked very tired and worn out. Shahjahan talked to her about her welfare and eventually asked her if Yunis was good to her. Ruby became very sad and told Shahjahan that Yunis was not a very nice person, that he was mean and unkind to her. Naz and her parents left Ruby's house and never saw her again. After this visit, Naz's father became sad and very quiet for a while

On the surface, Naz's mother Mumtaz may have

attributed all this to Naz's naseeb or destiny, but deep down she knew that she had made the wrong judgement about Yunis. This was particularly brought home to her when she heard Yunis's partner Ruby telling them that Yunis was not a good man. However, Naz told Mumtaz that it could happen in any marriage, even when a couple had courted for years beforehand. It could always happen that someone realised much later that they had married the wrong person. Sometimes, even when an extensive investigation has taken place, some people know how to hide their true personality.

Many years later, Mumtaz remarked that Naz was free in the true sense of the word, as she could come and go when and where she wanted. Mumtaz was courageous and farsighted, but she was also aware of the cultural and biradari constraints. Naz's sister Farah was also right to say that Naz would not have put up with the pressures from the biradari. Naz's family were fully aware that, as a child, Naz had a challenging personality and would question the traditional norms that she did not agree with. For example, she didn't accept her name and the reasons for it, so she changed it at the age of eight – from Naseeb to Naz.

When Naz had invited her parents to visit her in the UK, Shahjahan and Mumtaz were excited to make the trip. Some people in the biradari were a bit curious about the invitation. They told Naz's parents that now Naz was widowed, perhaps she wanted to remarry and had asked them to go there to give approval for her marriage or perhaps to choose a man for her. Shahjahan and Mumtaz were clever enough not to share this information with Naz but adopted a 'wait and see' policy.

During the week, Naz was at work whilst her parents would be waiting for the prospective husband to turn up. As friends would often turn up for a cup of tea or a meal, whenever there was a single man who turned up to The Gables, Naz's parents would not let him go. They would feed him and ask him all sorts of personal questions, thinking this must be a future husband for Naz. One time, a friend from the Ivory Coast came round when Naz was at work. Shahjahan and Mumtaz were convinced that this must be Naz's prospective husband. They made him stay in the house for hours, cooked for him, fed him, enquired about his family background, and grilled him about his personal habits. He was so relieved to see Naz when she came home from work, and he could not leave the house fast enough. Naz wondered that perhaps by grilling her friend in this way, her parents felt they were making up for the enquires they had not made before the marriage to Yunis.

One of Naz's friend, David, used to come round quite often for a meal and chat and he would sometimes do some DIY at The Gables. Shahjahan would talk to him for hours about cricket and other sports and Shahjahan became very fond of him. It was getting near the time for them to return to Pakistan, so they were getting desperate to meet their future son-in-law. In the end, Mumtaz expressed her and Shahjahan's preference for David and explained their intentions in showing so much interest in him. Naz told them that she had not asked them to approve a husband for her and she had no intentions of getting married again. One marriage was enough to put her off for life. It was nothing like that and they should relax before they went back. A few weeks later, Shahjahan and Mumtaz flew back to Pakistan, knowing that Naz and the children were okay.

Everything went back to routine. Naz was working in the social services area office in Cruddas Park, but was very tired and emotionally drained, thinking she wanted to do something different. Around that time, Naz was asked to go to the Head Office again, this time not to visit the Director but to see the training officer. The person was a lady in her fifties with a southern accent. There was quite a lot of prejudice in the North to people who spoke like that, but the woman turned out to be very helpful and introduced what was to be a significant change in Naz's life. She asked Naz if she wanted to do a master's degree in Social Work and Community Care. Naz was delighted to hear this. The training officer told her that the Social Services would second her and pay her fees as well as travelling expenses. The nearest course was at the University of Bradford, about two hours' drive from Gateshead. Naz went back to the office in Cruddas Park and told her senior and other colleagues. The senior, Mr Todd, was not convinced and told Naz it was highly unlikely. He said he didn't think it was easy for the Social Services Department to send someone on secondment, but no one had asked him. He seemed unhappy and didn't want to lose a member of staff, but she thought perhaps he felt his nose had been put out of joint. Nevertheless, in October 1983, Naz left Cruddas Park on a one-year secondment.

In May, Naz went for an interview at the University of Bradford. The University campus, right in the centre of the city, was vast and spread out in various departments. It had a fantastic library and student facilities. Naz drove from Gateshead to the University and arrived a few hours earlier than the interview time. She walked round the campus and had a good look around. She liked the multiracial and multicultural student community; it all looked very modern and very colourful with a very relaxed atmosphere. She liked it immediately and had the feeling that she would love it here. She still had some time before her interview, so she went to the students' café for a drink and to think about the interview. Naz bought herself a cup of coffee and sat down at a table that had two more empty chairs. As she sat down with her coffee, a young man with blond hair and blue eyes, very tall and slender and very relaxed, asked Naz if he could join her. Naz thought he must be one of the students and said that she had no problem with that. She had another look at the young man who had a very strong resemblance to the famous singer Sting. Sting was from Wallsend, Newcastle upon Tyne. Naz loved his song 'message in a bottle.' The young man started to talk to Naz and asked her all sorts of questions about what she was doing there, why social work, why this university, what books she read, and what she wanted to do in the future. Naz was so happy that someone was taking such an interest in her career and her training; she talked for more than an hour. All of a sudden, she realised that she must leave for her interview, or she would be very late. As Naz was about to rush off for her interview, the young man told her that there was no need to hurry and introduced himself as Trevor, one of the lecturers in the Social and Community work department. He told her that this had been the interview and that he would be very happy to give her a place on the course. Naz was a bit embarrassed and started to think back on the frank and candid conversation they had had, but she was delighted to secure a place on the course.

The course was taught two days a week with the rest of the time in private study, so Naz could travel to Bradford on Monday mornings and come back on Tuesday evenings. This meant that for now, she would only need to stay away on Monday nights, but in any case, Raza was already twenty years old by this time, Omer was nineteen, and Rumi was fifteen. One of Naz's brothers also came to stay with the children for a few months to help. After two terms, Naz stayed at home and did her research and wrote her dissertation. She enjoyed her time in Bradford. She loved the teaching and learning new theories, and the interaction with other students. The course leaned more towards left wing politics, which Naz enjoyed very much. She met students from all over the country and got to know the local politics, which was interesting as well as very informative.

Bradford had a very large Pakistani community. They had arrived from the rural Pakistan in the 1950s and 1960s to work in the cotton mills in the North of Britain. The raw material for these mills came from Pakistan and was made into cotton in Bradford. The Pakistani community who came to Bradford and the surrounding area spoke their own dialect and had their own culture, and their issues and problems were often unique to that community. The first generation worked in the mills but when the mills closed, the second generation found different employment.

Naz would have liked to have spent more time in the university and getting to know this community, but due to her responsibilities at home, she could not do so. The research and writing of her thesis was very hard work, but it was very rewarding in the end.

In September 1984, Naz went back to the Social Services Department. This time, she was working in Community Services where she developed new projects in the community. As well as other projects, Naz wanted to set up a support group for Asian women who were working within the Council and in voluntary organisations. She knew from her own experience working for the City Council that there were no support groups and no role models, and she felt isolated. She thought that it was important to have a support group which would help the women who were already working and encourage other women to enter the work force. It was decided that the group would be called Saheli, which in Urdu and Punjabi means female friend. To form and run the group was harder than Naz thought it was going to be. Asking for time out for the meetings to the various organisations was the easiest part. The most difficult bit was setting up the guidelines and strategies, and get everyone agreeing to them. The problem was that not all the Asian women came from the same part of South Asia and they all had different cultural backgrounds and languages. They came from various family, economic, and educational backgrounds. The main issue was that their views, life experiences, and concepts of racism and sexism were very different from each other. The aim was very clear, to support each other and share information and experiences, to gain confidence and move on, but there was a lack of confidence within themselves and in each other. Cliques formed and lots of infighting went on, which made it very difficult to have fruitful discussion or make decisions. As Naz had just come out of Bradford University, where women were radical and outspoken, she found it very hard to run the group. One of the issues for some Asian women was that the group should also include white women. Naz thought that this would defeat the whole objective of setting up the group, so she put her foot down and rejected the idea outright. This created some resentment against Naz, and some women thought she was too radical. There were so many different types of women, different cultures and values, that it was difficult to have a consensus about the aims. But at least it started debates, and the Saheli group continued to run, although in a different shape and with a different ideology than it had begun with. After a couple of years, Naz moved to a different job.

Naz came back from Bradford University at the same time as the miners' strike was taking place, 1984 to 1985, and she had changed significantly. She started to think about the political context of her work and some of the government policies that were creating real social problems. Some concerned her greatly, like Margaret Thatcher's policy of withdrawing free school milk from children, which had started much earlier but was especially hard for the families who were genuinely in need of the milk. Then there was the miners' strike and the erosion of trade union rights. Despite a lot of support, the strike was lost and the mining villages became ghost towns with high unemployment, especially for young people. Naz was still working on the projects in the Family Service Unit, Law Centre, and the Credit Union, but she started to think she was only touching the tip of the iceberg. Voluntary and statutory organisations were not changing people's lives, only helping them to survive within the status quo. The miners' strike had such a big impact on Naz's life that she wanted to work for real change in people's lives. She was disillusioned with social work and started to think about radical social work and education, which she believed could bring real change to people's lives.

In the North, the 'ghost' towns were gloomy places to live in. Some people moved out to find new jobs, but others stayed there and remained unemployed. Naz found it depressing and frightening to see the pits closed. The shops, some schools and other civic facilities were shutting down. These areas started to look like derelict mountains of rubbish. Naz heard that some older miners still went to the mines in the morning and had a shower there with the special miners' soap. This was probably partly a habit and partly for the company.

Naz remembered when the small towns and villages were busy with little food shops, green grocers, ice cream shops and, of course, the fish and chip shops that were always 'alive and kicking.' Naz remembered that before the mines closed, she once went to a working men's club in Ashington. All the lasses were sitting in one corner and all the lads in another corner playing dominoes. This gender separation reminded Naz of Pakistan where men and women sit separately. She noticed when one husband got up to go to the bar, he would shout, "Same pet?" and she would reply, "Aye". Then he would buy a pint for himself and half for his wife, but also have a short for himself whilst his wife was not looking. Later, the wife would send a friend to the bar and give her the money to buy her a short. This went on all evening until the couple were leaving the club totally drunk. Naz heard one husband saying to his wife that he wished he had had what she had had, and she replied, "Aye". Naz could not help thinking that this couple must have been married for at least forty years and wondered how often they had played this game.

Northumberland's beautiful beaches are stunning with miles and miles of golden sand, which were always exciting for Naz. One of the beaches, which was Naz and the children's favourite, was Druridge Bay. They used to go there with their cocker spaniel dog called Henry, and have a lot of fun. Around this time, the Northumberland Council decided to build a power station near Druridge Bay. Some people started to protest against this plan, and within a few weeks, the protests grew bigger, into hundreds of people. Naz also joined the protest. The protesters would spend all weekend on the beach, including overnight. They were all young people, and they would have a bonfire people and would bring food and drinks to share with each other. Some people would bring their children. Naz would take her children and food for them and sometimes big blankets to wrap themselves in. Raza would bring his girlfriend with him.

Naz had a friend called Steve, who was in a wheelchair. One night, Steve turned up in the middle of the night, rolling in his wheelchair and coming through the sand dunes. Everyone was surprised and shocked by how he had managed to get there. This gave everyone a lot of courage and confidence to carry on protesting. It was a lot of fun, but people also felt they were doing this for a worthy cause. After a lot of protesting and a lot of time, sometimes on the cold and windy beach, Northumberland Council withdrew its plan to build a power station.

Chapter 13

Family Change

Naz's children were getting fed up with Bohemian life and the happy-go-lucky lifestyle. Their mother was working all week and then either attending union meetings or voluntary organisation meetings in the evenings and weekends. She was also taking out her clients' children to the beach or to eat out. Her own children were getting older and seeing other households and wanted to have a life like most families in the area where mum stayed at home and father worked. The children saw nothing like this. Naz was enjoying her freedom and her work, both voluntary and statutory, and feeling her worth in society.

As the children got into their teens and late teens and were growing up, issues of independence began to emerge. They wanted to leave home. Omer was undertaking a foundation course in fashion design and a few months after finishing the course, he decided to leave home and move to London. During the course, he met a beautiful girl called Lila and brought her home. The whole family fell in love with her. Lila loved The Gables, particularly the Victorian chapatti flour bin, which Naz had bought from the second-hand shop. Forty years later, Lila is still a best friend of the family. Omer thought he would be happier in London and would have more opportunities there because it was more multiracial and multicultural. Raza was also unsettled, moving in and out of the house. Sometimes he would move out and go and stay with friends. Then he would move back home. As the oldest child in the family, he was more grown up. He was more rooted in Geordie culture but also felt something of an outsider, possibly because of his background, colour, the Bohemian lifestyle of the family, or perhaps because he came from a single-parent household. He tried very hard to be an insider rather than an outsider, trying hard to be one of the boys. Rumi was also fighting to leave home, her argument being that all her friends had left home, so why couldn't she leave home? Naz told her she could leave home when she finished her A-levels.

Around this time, Naz had an offer from Newcastle Polytechnic to teach part time on the social work course. After a year or so, a full-time job came up, which Naz applied for and was offered the post of lecturer. For Naz, this was a chance to provide opportunities for women like her, women who did not have opportunities in their earlier lives. She set about doing this and succeeded in encouraging women from the Asian community to apply for the course. They saw Naz as a role model and identified with her.

In the Polytechnic, Naz worked with a group of women

lecturers teaching on the course. She thought they were brilliant, clever and supportive and they gave her confidence. She was inspired and encouraged by them to develop ideas to teach to the students. There was a special buzz being around these women, and Naz was learning and developing new ideas all the time. She bought her first Amstrad computer and started to type her own work. It was like magic. It was the first time that Naz had felt her ideas were listened to and valued. She could discuss ideas openly and relate them to her own experiences, especially issues in social policy, which became a particular interest.

Naz felt the notion of sisterhood had come alive for her and she was very pleased to be a part of this group. After all the years living in this country, she had missed the type of support and companionship of other women which she had had in Pakistan. Naz had tried to find a similar sort of support in the Saheli group, but had not been able to find this due to professional jealousies and the lack of confidence of the women involved. It also may have been due to the fact that many of these women had been second generation and had born and grown up in Britain. Within modern feminism at that time, there was a type of approach often called 'women's groups,' but for Naz, this was something very old and natural. She always thought her female friends in Britain really did not understand the notion of sisterhood. One of the reasons could be that living as a couple or a couple and their children in a nuclear family made them become more of an independent unit. At the time, Naz noticed that female friends put a sexual partner first, that a female platonic relationship was never on the same par as the sexual relationship. Naz also thought that in courtship, love, and marriage, women tended to compete, which brought about mistrust and suspicion. In arranged marriages, there was less chance of this and perhaps the reason why women stick together more. When Naz was growing up in Pakistan, women and girls had very a strong bond. They shared everything with their female friends and looked for support from them, as well as from other female relatives. The notion of sisterhood was very strong. For example, when women got pregnant, their female friends or other females in the family, like their mother or mother-in-law, would be the first to know. Also, women preferred a female friend or a relative with them at the time of childbirth. When men in Britain started to be present at the birth of their child, it could sometimes cause problems if a woman preferred to have only women at the birth and not the partner. More often, in families in Pakistan, women would eat together and men would eat separately. Similarly, women and girls would go out together often at weddings and funerals. However, things have also changed in Pakistan with more modern trends and some developing a nuclear family pattern. It is still the same for most Asian women and some, having tried the nuclear family, find that it hasn't worked for them.

Whilst at the Polytechnic, Naz was asked to join the national editorial group of the journal *Critical Social Policy*, a quarterly peer-reviewed academic journal that publishes articles in the field of political science. She was delighted and thought it was an absolute privilege to read the articles, people's work from all over the UK. She was eager to meet people in the editorial group, men and women, most of whom had written and published several books and articles. She would go regularly to London to meet with the group and loved the heated discussion and rigorous reviews of the articles. In this circle, Naz felt her opinions and views were valued and she would travel back to Newcastle mentally fulfilled and satisfied.

The time came when Rumi finished her A-levels and she was ready to leave home. Naz felt it was okay to let her go and knew that if she stopped her now, Naz's life would not be worth living, so it would be best to let her go! Rumi brought a white van, loaded up her stuff and, at nineteen years old, left to live independently, sharing a flat in Newcastle with friends.

Now they had all left home (Raza more out than in), Naz was alone in The Gables. She did not have the empty nest feelings that she had heard and read about, or feel redundant as a mother. She felt happy to be on her own and could do what she wanted to do for herself without the extra chores of looking after the family. At the same time, she started to feel guilty that she was living in such a big house on her own and some people didn't have a roof over their head, so she started to think about selling The Gables and giving her money to more deserving people.

She also started to think about leaving Newcastle and moving south, partly to live in warmer weather and partly to meet more people from her own background. Newcastle had been a very good for her and the city had provided her with a lot of opportunities. She had made some friends for life and raised her three children there. Naz felt great affection and love for the city and the people of the city. On the other hand, the city was also starting to feel restrictive. Naz had been the only Asian woman as a student, then a social worker, and now a lecturer. In these situations, it felt to Naz as though she had a tokenistic value - either very good or very bad. The Asian community was very small and everyone had their own views and opinions about her. Some women wanted to be like her, but they couldn't be like her and other disliked her for what she represented. They could not decide whether she was good or bad. Independent and successful Pakistani woman struggled amongst themselves, so things remained unresolved. Naz could feel that tension.

Naz put The Gables on the market and applied for a job at Warwick University and at West London Institute of Higher Education (WLIHE, as everyone called it). Omer was pushing Naz to go to London, and he kept telling her that she would be very happy in London. Eventually Naz sold The Gables and at the same time, was offered a lecturer post at WLIHE. Naz knew a Pakistani woman called Ruby in West London who offered Naz a room to stay when she moved to London. A few months earlier, Ruby's young daughter had been murdered in very brutal circumstances and Ruby was understandably in shock from this. She lived on her own and Naz thought that Ruby could do with someone to share her grief.

The plan for the money from the sale of The Gables was to give most of it away. Some of the money was given to Naz's family to buy a house in Rawalpindi and some was given to family and friends. The rest, Naz decided to give to the Afghan refugees who were in Islamabad. One very good old friend, Anne, also gave money for the Naz's Afghan refugee project. Following the Soviet Union's invasion of Afghanistan, it is estimated that three to four million Afghanis went to Pakistan. Some who had family or friendship connections were taken in, others lived in camps outside Islamabad. As Naz had been homeless herself and in similar difficult circumstances, she thought she would give something back to this community with the proceeds from The Gables and the money from her friend Anne.

In the summer of 1988, Raza offered to drive Naz to London, and they left Newcastle in a small Ford Fiesta with her Amstrad and a few clothes. The rest of the stuff went into storage in Newcastle. The Fiesta broke down several times on the motorway and it was lucky that Raza was there to help. After a week, Naz left her Fiesta and her Amstrad outside Ruby's house, said goodbye to Ruby and left for Rawalpindi to stay with her family. Naz did not tell anyone in the family in Rawalpindi about her plan to distribute money amongst the refugees except for her cousin, who was going to drive her to Islamabad. The reason for not telling her family was that in Pakistan, everyone has an opinion and gives advice. Naz thought they would confuse her, and that therefore she would just go ahead and do what she had planned.

On the morning that she had planned to drive to the refugee camp in Islamabad (not a long distance), Naz picked up her chador; as she was going to the Afghan refugee camp, she thought she should cover herself. However, in Pakistan, as soon as you pick up your chador, members of the family will walk out of the door with you without feeling the need to ask if you'd like them to come along. Sometimes when you are walking and you have walked a long way, you turn round and will see some family members following you. The same thing happens to men, but men only follow men. Women will only follow men if they know exactly where the man is going (e.g., family visits or shopping) then they will follow them, and if it is men's business, then the women will not follow them. Naz always found this irritating because in England she went everywhere on her own. However, she never said anything because she knew that no one meant any harm and that it was to do with closeness and just wanting to be with someone whom you love and care about.

As soon as Naz and her driver cousin sat in the car, her two other male cousins and a nephew all over six feet tall came and sat in the back seat. Her cousins knew where the refugees' camps were. They told Naz that all the refugee men left home in the morning to look for jobs and only women and children would be in the camp. Naz thought this was better as she would be able to talk to the women and give each household enough money to buy food supplies for one month.

Out of respect, Naz's cousins decided to stay in the car and wait for Naz because there were no men in the camp. Naz went into the first tent where an old woman was sitting. Naz inquired about her welfare, talked to her for a few minutes, and gave her the money. The same thing happened in the next tent, which had a young woman with children, and Naz gave her the envelope with money. By the time Naz was in the third tent, she heard a lot of voices outside. When she looked outside the tent, she saw a big crowd running towards her. The women dragged her out of the tent, threw her in the bushes and started to pull all the money from her bag. Naz tried to resist, but there were more than twenty women, and the money was scattered everywhere. Naz had some money in her hand, which she was about to give to the third family. She made a tight fist around it, but the women forced her fist open and took that money as well. Naz was lying on her back in the bushes with big thorns. Her back hurt, she was bleeding from the scratches, and she felt her fingers were broken. Her chador was nowhere in sight, and her clothes were torn. Naz's cousins and the nephew had heard the screaming, shouting and loud noise coming from the women and they came over, lifted Naz out the bushes and threw her in the car. They all got in and started to drive away but as they started to move, men turned up within minutes and tried to stop the car by trying to stand in the front or following on motorbikes. Eventually, they got home and when the rest of the family saw Naz, they became very concerned. Her sister and nieces got the shower ready for her and brought her clean clothes to change. When they heard the story, they all said she should have asked them, and they would have told her about several charity organisations for refugees. They also laughed at Naz and said she had become too English. Didn't she remember that if anyone was distributing cooked rice (which was a well-known tradition in Pakistan) in this country, there was such a big skirmishing and scuffling in the crowds that grown-up men hesitated to go there. And Naz hadn't had rice, she had been distributing real money!

Naz realised that whenever she went to Pakistan, people said she had become too English, though she spoke perfect Punjabi and Urdu, and her village dialect better than the new generation. Naz noticed that, when she went to the local market, even the market sellers tried to speak English with her. She was always intrigued by this. Once she asked her sister why it was that whenever she came to Pakistan, even people in the street thought she was a foreigner. She wore clothes like everyone else and always made sure she had her chador and covered her head like everyone in the street. Her sister told her it was not only wearing the chador and covering the head but the way she wore the chador and walked while wearing the chador, which was very different from the local women. The street traders especially are very canny. As soon as they saw someone like her, they knew she would pay them a good price because she didn't know how to haggle. Her sister also said no Pakistani woman would walk into a refugee camp with the whole lot of money. Naz was shocked and shaken to hear this but fortunately, her other injuries were superficial.

On one hand, she felt sad to think that she was a foreigner wherever she went, but on the other, she felt lucky to belong to several cultures and communities. Being an outsider and living on the periphery meant you had to learn a lot more and had to make great efforts to achieve anything in life. Naz thought that perhaps she had always been like this. She had always felt different. Perhaps her mother, who was a shrewd woman, recognised this in Naz and sent her away. Naz often wondered whether, had she married and lived in

Pakistan, would she have been able to live the life her sister and other female relatives were living? Would she be a dutiful wife and mother? Would she have been able to put up with the clan and all the issues and pressures from the extended family? Naz's sister always told Naz that she didn't think Naz could have put up with all the pressures of living in a very big family with patriarchal practices. Naz's mother, Mumtaz, used to say the same to her, that she was free in the true meaning of the word. Mumtaz also said she herself that could not have survived if she had not had a very good man for her husband, Naz's father. She had wanted to be a musician, like her father, Wilayet Shah, but he was sent to Singapore and had to leave the family. Naz wondered whether Mumtaz had also had some ambivalence about her own naseeb, because her own life might have been very different if she had lived with her father. There was some contradiction in both their lives - destiny or free will?

Naz used to go back to Rawalpindi in the summer and while she was there, her sister and all her female friends would move in with her. They would talk, laugh, play games, go out to eat, go to the cinema and visit gardens. The friends' husbands and sons used to say that when Aunty Naz was there, the least of the problem would be that they would not have home cooking because the females would be with Naz, and the worst was that by the time Aunty Naz went back, one or two of her friends would be asking for divorce!

Naz was always interested in Sufism. She would visit their shrines while in Pakistan and would see many women sitting reading the Quran. People do this for the benefit of the owner of the shrine. Naz would gather the women under a tree and sit cross-legged on the floor, reading the translation of the Quran, especially the parts relating to women's rights. Naz could not help making comparisons with teaching feminism in England.

When Naz returned to London after her visit to Pakistan, she had hoped to stay with her friend Ruby as planned. However, Ruby was still very disturbed; she had forgotten that she had promised a room to Naz, and when she saw her she failed to recognise her. She threw her stuff out and started to scream at shout at her. Naz could understand her grief, so she picked her stuff up to load it into the little Fiesta, but Ruby had slashed the tyres. So, once again, Naz found herself penniless and homeless. After Naz had her car fixed, she drove to WLIHE and parked in the car park because it was summer and not many people were around. She decided to sleep in the car for a few days until she could find a place to live. Naz, her Amstrad and her Fiesta lived in WLIHE's car park for a few days until she found a room in Chiswick with someone she knew.

The West London Institute of Higher Education (WLIHE) was by the river and near Richmond. Naz worked in a very picturesque setting, a Victorian building with gardens and mature trees all round. When Naz had first come for her interview, she had fallen in love with the place. There was a lecture hall in an old Victorian church, which was very quaint. Naz thought her ancestors would be turning in their graves to see her standing in church giving lectures.

After moving to Chiswick, Naz started exploring

London at weekends. She would go to places like art galleries, theatres, films, various exhibitions, music venues and to Southall and flower markets. Omer would come and meet her and they would go out together and have dinner. This was the first time in her life that she was totally living on her own. She loved every minute of living in London and met several women like herself. She loved the fact that she was on her own with no responsibilities, and no one to worry about anymore.

The work at WLIHE was also very good. Her colleagues were brilliant and very relaxed. She loved the fact that the staff group was multiracial and that people were aware and sensitive regarding race and gender issues. Naz was made welcome; people were very helpful and made sure that she was introduced into the WLIHE culture. Naz loved the atmosphere and meeting various people through teaching and practice placements.

The best thing about the social work courses was that the student group was totally multiracial. Naz loved to see the students whose parents or grandparents came from different backgrounds like Africa, the West Indies, Ethiopia, South Africa as well as local people studying on the courses. Naz felt very comfortable with these students. She enjoyed the discussions and sharing experiences of families, immigration, and education. Naz thought she had natural empathy with these students because she herself had been through some similar experiences. One of the things that Naz was very keen on was that women and particularly black students, took an interest in social policy. She thought it was important for these students to have a good grasp of how opinions are formed, and how laws got passed in Parliament and were implemented in society. Formerly, students tended to think of social policy as a dry subject but gradually, they started to think of it as relating closely to their own, and to their clients', day-to-day lives.

In 1988/89, the interest rate was very high on mortgages, something like 15% to 17%. This meant that it was impossible for Naz to borrow money or buy a flat so she could only rent rooms. It also meant that the market was saturated with a lot of rooms to rent, and that therefore some properties were going into negative equity. Naz found another room in Chiswick. Her landlady Sarah was happy to sacrifice her bedroom to Naz, and she herself moved into her living room. Because the flat was so small and cramped, Naz spent a lot of time at work during the day and out in the evenings. After a few months, this started to get very tiring.

The other thing about the flat was that, apart from being very small, there was no cooker or even any cooking facilities, not even a toaster. The reason for this was that Sarah only believed in eating raw food. She had been brought up on a farm and her argument was that all the animals on the farm never cooked anything, so why should humans? Tea and coffee were acceptable, so there was a kettle available. Naz had not noticed that there was no cooker when she agreed to rent the place; as far as she was concerned, one buys the cooker before the home. For Naz, life revolved around cooking, eating, inviting friends over and feeding them. Or feeding anyone who pops in. The cooker was the focal point of the home. A cooker-less home did not feel like a home.

It took Naz some time for it to sink in that there was no cooker in the flat. Sarah was happy to munch away on cornflakes, muesli or anything else she could eat cold, whereas Naz was used to cooking fried eggs, jam on toast or omelette with green chillies, onions, green coriander and paratha on Sundays. In the beginning, Naz would go on Chiswick High Road to have breakfast and evening meals, but it got very expensive to eat out twice a day and no one could make omelette and paratha like her. She was longing for her own food and her own cooking. Sometimes she would go to Southall to eat all the spices she could, but it was not sustainable. So, she decided to move out and look for a proper home.

Chapter 14

Change

As Naz started to think about a new flat to rent, a very good colleague at WLIHE, Jan, offered Naz accommodation in her home. Jan had a very big house in St Margaret's, which had several rooms, a large kitchen (with a cooker), a lovely conservatory, a big garden and a flat at the top. She lived with her two very beautiful children, one aged around twelve and the other ten. They were very middle class and well behaved. Both children were delightful and charming. Naz was offered the complete top flat with no rent, just free of charge. The house was close to work, which made life very easy, plus Jan and the children were very easy going as well as good company. The family also had a Bohemian lifestyle, similar to that of Naz and her children when they had lived at The Gables. However, there was a big difference in that this family was very well off, not like Naz and her family - struggling Bohemians. Naz liked the easy-going lifestyle, but what surprised her was that they never cooked. As far as Naz was concerned, food shopping, cooking, and eating together, was a central part of life. If you were poor, you bought cheaper cuts of meat and went to the market to buy cheaper fruits and vegetables to cook for the family. First, Naz thought it was a London thing, but later she understood that it was Jan's thing. When you are poor, all you think about is food, so you spend your time thinking, hunting, and preparing the food. When Naz worked in Cruddas Park as a social worker, she used to make sure that her clients' children were eating well and were not malnourished. Similarly, when Naz and the children had lived together, Naz had always started planning what to cook her family at the end of the working day.

In this house, it wasn't that they didn't eat, they just didn't cook, and the food would be delivered from Harrods. A very fancy van would arrive in front of the door and very fancy food would be delivered. Naz had never seen food like this before, let alone eaten it. The staff from Harrods would come into the house and put the food in the fridge and the cupboards. Sometimes, the family would get food delivered from the local take-away. The children and Jan would order whatever each of them felt like eating. The other thing Naz noticed was that nobody did any housework, which she had thought was central to most households. Naz reflected on when she lived with her children; certain bits of housework were allocated to the children, like cleaning their bedrooms, and taking turns to wash the dishes and clean the floors. Thinking back, she wondered whether she had been unkind to make them do housework at a young age, like her mother had with her. On the other hand, perhaps it was not a bad thing to get them doing things at an early age to help them learn. In this house, it was nothing like that. There was a cleaning lady who would come over three or four times a week. She would make herself a cup of coffee, hang around for a few hours, sometimes chat with anyone who was around, and then leave. Naz thought this was very strange as she never saw her doing any housework. Why did the cleaning lady not clean? This was all very new to Naz.

The good thing was that Naz could do anything she wanted to do in the house. There were no restrictions of any kind. Sometimes Naz would shop and cook and invite her son Omer, who lived in the area, and whoever else was in the house, to eat with them. That would be a very nice evening. The children and Jan would not always be around to eat together, and Naz had to clean the kitchen before starting any cooking, so that sometimes took a lot of time. This lifestyle was very new for Naz, but after living there for a few months, she started to understand a bit, especially when some of the visitors came to see Jan and the children. The visitors were familiar faces, people she had seen on television, and Naz recognised some as serving ministers in the government. It started to make sense, confirmed one day when Jan's mother rang to speak to her daughter and Jan was out. Naz told her that she was a lodger and happy to take a message. The message was that Prince Charles was coming to tea and she couldn't find the flagstaff to put the flag up. Naz then realised that Jan was not just middle class but upper class, which she had kept a secret from her colleagues and perhaps others. Although Naz had read about the class system and written about it, she had never lived with it, never experienced it that close. But Naz thoroughly enjoyed Jan's generosity, her intellect, and her wonderful nature. This was a very memorable period in Naz's life.

Omer was growing up to be a very handsome young man. He was very tall and slender, like Naz. And like Naz, his skin complexion was a wheat colour that got darker in the summer. Raza and Rumi had skin more like their father, more on the paler side. Naz and Omer went out a lot together and enjoyed each other's company. Omer introduced her to all his favourite places in London and together they would eat and drink and laugh a lot. Omer stopped calling her mum or mother, like they all used to call her in Gateshead. He started to call her by her name and they became more like friends than mother and son. He wore very fashionable clothes and started to earn some money by doing modelling now and then. He also worked in fashion houses and his aim was to secure a place on a fashion course at Central Saint Martins - University of the Arts, London. Omer would take Naz to these 'way out' shops in London and push her to buy unconventional clothes and shoes and try them on in the shop. Naz would never in her dreams have thought she would be wearing such clothes, like a very tight short skirt and stiletto heels. They would come out of shops laughing but not buying the outrageous clothes. Raza and Rumi never did anything like this. Naz was their mother, and they liked her the way she was. Omer was quite possessive about Naz and always told her to not invite Raza and Rumi to come to London because they would only call her mother in public. However, she wanted to spend time with all her children. Omer persuaded her to buy her own flat and pay the mortgage together so that they could cook their own food and eat together. Jan was not sure that Naz should do that as she thought the interest rate was so high that Naz would not be able to pay the mortgage. Naz later found out that Jan was right, but after six very interesting months of living with her, Naz moved out.

Omer and Naz found a very small two bedroomed flat in Twickenham. The kitchen and bathroom were a reasonable size, but the second bedroom was very small. Naz got all her stuff from The Gables out of storage and when Omer saw it all, he threw half of it out, saying that it was too big for the flat and too old-fashioned. He decorated the flat and made curtains and cushion covers. He would tie his head with a red scarf and sit with his sewing machine. Naz did not mind his outrageous suggestions, whether it was to do with decorating or inviting friends. She loved the fact that Omer was living with her in London. Every day after finishing work, Naz would pick up Omer's favourite food and drinks and they would cook together and eat. She missed the other two children as well, but she knew they were busy and she would see them soon. Omer was very self assured and full of confidence, sometimes to the point of arrogance, but Naz thought it was just his youth. Once, he was working in a fashion shop and a lady customer tried on a dress and asked him if the dress suited her. He told her that it didn't suit her and when the owner of the shop heard this, she sacked him. He would regularly take risks, whether it was to do with things like walking on the road, or more serious things such as putting his job on the line. He would also go swimming in the nearby river every morning; Naz would be sitting on the bank terrified, holding her breath, waiting for him to return safely. She could only breathe again after she saw him coming out of the water, and then they would have breakfast.

Naz was thoroughly enjoying her job at WLIHE. She loved the students and the staff, and the location was one of the best in London. She enjoyed travelling from one end of London to the other to visit students on their placements and she enjoyed meeting different people and working with them. Naz thought she was learning so much from all these people. Most of the students were from families of Caribbean and Africa origin, but there were hardly any from the Asian community. She found that there were a lot of Asian workers who were doing a great job in the community. For example, in day care, working almost as unqualified social workers. Their work was not recognised, and they were also low paid due to a lack of formal qualifications. Naz thought it might be a good idea to use her private study time – half a day each week – to recruit some of these people onto an Access Course so that they could afterwards enrol on professional social work courses.

She got in touch with the Extra-Mural Studies Department at the University of London and learned how to set up an Access to Social Work Course. The atmosphere at WLIHE was flexible, so Naz did not have to go through red tape to do what she wanted to do. She put together a one-year access course and at the end of the course, students were awarded a certificate from the University of London, making them eligible to apply for a social work course. Every year, the course was run in Southall at various venues, like community centres, church halls and schools. Most students were mature and from Asian and Afro-Caribbean backgrounds. All the students had a wealth of experience and were doing much needed work in the community, either on a one-to-one basis or in groups, day centres or in residential settings. Naz loved teaching these students as they were enthusiastic and very hard working. One of the best things was that Naz asked other colleagues from her department to teach their subjects on the Access course in Southall. Her colleagues were kind enough to give up their study time to do this. Jack taught criminology, and the students loved the subject and his personality. Ruth taught sexuality and was enthusiastic and eager to teach those students with Naz. Her class was in the community centre with strict time limits and it was always pushed for time. One time, the room was booked after Ruth's class for the community elders' meeting. Ruth and Naz were teaching together, and the students were all charged up because Naz and Ruth were asking them to shout out all the words used for sex and sexuality. Students were shouting out words in English, which Ruth wrote on the whiteboard and Naz was writing the words students were shouting in Urdu and Punjabi, which sound much worse than English on the same whiteboard. The purpose of this exercise was to demonstrate how all these words, whichever language they were in, were derogatory to women. At the end of the discussion, Naz heard the Asian elders standing outside the door trying to get in. Naz and Ruth were trying very hard to clean the white board with water and a sponge, but the words were not coming off. Naz stood in the door, blocking the elders so that Ruth could clean the board. By this time, the students also realised the severity of the situation, so they brought more sponges and more water. In the end, the words became slightly blurred and Naz moved away from the door to let the elders in.

After a year or so, in 1990, Omer started to get bored living with Naz. All his friends were in North London, and he wanted to be with them. It was difficult for him to live in Twickenham and spend time with his friends in Stoke Newington or in Islington, so he decided to move out. After that, Naz started to find it very hard to pay the mortgage. Most of her lecturer's salary was spent paying the mortgage and the bills every month, so she had to borrow money from the bank to live. She thought very hard about how to get out of the situation, though she kept on paying the mortgage and the bills, but the bank overdraft was increasing monthly. This situation was getting more and more stressful by the day. Naz mentioned her situation to a friend and colleague, Ann, who told Naz that she has a two bedroomed flat in Putney, which she rented to nurses who were soon leaving. Naz was delighted with the offer of a rented flat and the rent was half the money she was paying for the mortgage, so she decided to move into the flat in 1991. Naz went to the building society to hand over the keys of her flat and they took them without a word.

Naz did not have the money to pay for the removal van, and Raza and Omer were not available to help her to move, so Rumi came down from Newcastle. Naz and Rumi loaded a hired van and carried a washing machine downstairs to load onto it. Looking back, it was a big mistake. It was unbelievably hard and, in the end, it was not worth it because the washing machine didn't work when they got there. The flat in Putney was a two-bedroom, first-floor flat in a very nice area. It was a Victorian flat which needed modernisation but would be suitable for the next few years. The flat had lovely big windows with a view of the gardens from the back and front. Ann lived quite nearby, so Naz also had a friend and a colleague who lived close to her.

WLIHE became a constituent college of Brunel University and the pressure started to mount on staff to do a PhD, as well as publish as much as possible. That meant that there was less time to spend directly with students, like reduced time for seminars and tutorials. Naz always thought the good thing about teaching at WLIHE was about spending time with students, both formally and informally. This became less of a priority and more emphasis was placed on research and PhDs.

Naz started to discuss her options for her research and, as she had always been interested in community care, she thought she would do a comparative study of community care in Britain and Pakistan.

She did a literature search about the integration of health and community care in Britain, which was limited at that time and still is, and then one about a part of Pakistan called Gilgit. In the summer of 1992, Naz went to Gilgit to do some research.

Gilgit is the capital city of Gilgit-Baltistan and is quite a unique place. The city is in a broad valley near the confluence of the Gilgit River and Hunza River. The region of Gilgit-Baltistan lies in the very north of Pakistan, about 600km from Rawalpindi, in the foothills of the Himalayan Mountains. It is situated on the old Silk Road. It forms the northern part of the larger Kashmir region and is called 'the roof of the world' because of its mountains. Its boundaries touch China to the east and northeast, and India to the southeast. The Hunza Valley, through which the Hunza River flows, is known as heaven on earth, famous for its fruits. Hunza dried apricots are sold all over the world. An important factor in this region is that people live until a 'ripe old age' and stay healthy. Because of its location, the air and water are very clean. When tourists bring bottles of water with them, and then throw the empty bottles away, the local children fill them with Hunza water, considered far superior to what was originally in the bottles, and sell it back to them.

All the regions in Pakistan are very different from each other, but Gilgit-Baltistan is particularly different because of its remote location and culture. Buses do run to Gilgit, but usually people travel there by air from Islamabad. In the winter, there are fewer flights due to the low clouds and high mountains. The local people are different in appearance physically as well as in their language, clothes, culture and lifestyle. Most of Gilgit's community are followers of Prince Aga Khan and belong to the Shia religion. The majority of the people are educated and the literacy rate is very high among young people. Young people go to Agha Khan University in Karachi, which is in the far south of Pakistan, but after completing their education, almost all of them return to Gilgit to serve their community. Women and men mix freely and there is no concept of purdah. There are no mosques but community centres instead. Lots of activities – both for adults and children – take place in the community centres. Women feel safe in these communities and work side by side with the men, whether it is in the community or in the fields or offices.

Naz enjoyed doing the research in Gilgit. She liked their systems of community care and thought that she would look at their working patterns to see what she could learn. She stayed in a big house which was like a guest house but totally empty. Women in a nearby house took on the responsibility of supplying cooked meals, which worked well. All the food was local and very simple, mostly vegetables and fruits. On a very rare occasion, they would slaughter a yak, which is a buffalo-like animal living in the Himalayan Mountains. People live very simple lives and without many luxuries, like cars, television, fancy shoes and clothes, which many in the West regard as necessities. Naz visited community centres, maternity centres, and antenatal clinics and saw health visitors walking for miles to see women, which impressed her very much. Despite how very difficult the terrain was and very harsh winters, the workers visited their patients miles away from the office. Naz saw that all the services were seamless. The professionals talked to each other regularly despite there being no telephones at the time. Naz made lots of notes and took a video camera with her. She made a film and took lots of video clips. After finishing her research in Gilgit, Naz came back to Rawalpindi to fly back to London.

During that time, for perhaps a year or so, Naz did not see Omer very much. Partly she was very busy, and partly he was not around. He stayed in Paris for a while and would send a card from France or sometimes from Spain. Then he wrote to say he had become a student at Central Saint Martin's and felt like a king now; he said that the teachers loved him and the other students adored him. Naz was missing him desperately and wanted to see him. Raza and Rumi were both quite busy and had not seen him for a while, either. Omer's childhood friends, Lila and George, were both in London now, but they complained to Naz that Omer had made new friends in London and did not see them anymore.

Around Easter 1992, Naz had caught up with Omer and they had arranged that he would come to her flat for a meal. Naz cooked for both of them and waited for him, but he was very late, so she had the meal and decided to mark some students' assignments. She went downstairs to get the students' work out of the car boot and when she looked around, Omer was standing behind her. He never said why he was late and Naz did not ask him. She tried to serve him the food, but he said he would help himself. They were talking while he was eating and Naz asked him about Saint Martin's. Omer told Naz about his interview there and said that most of the people who came out of the interview had left, almost crying. He said when he was interviewed, they all laughed so much it didn't seem like an interview. After Omer left, Naz started to think about her children and felt very proud that they were all doing so well. She thought the bad times were over and all the struggle and tough times were behind her. This was the first time as an adult that she had felt genuine contentment deep inside – this was it! She felt like she had built the Titanic.

Raza was working for Oxfam and turned out to be a hardworking and responsible young man. He was very handsome and had a very nice girlfriend who was loved by the entire family. He had a charming and engaging personality, so was popular with his colleagues. He enjoyed raising funds for Oxfam and looked forward to making his mark for this worthy cause. He was heading towards a successful career and building his future. Raza was a first-born child, and Naz was particularly close to him as her first born; he was equally loved by his mother and grandparents (Naz's parents). She was proud of the sensitive and caring person that he had become. This was Naz then, looking forward to having grandchildren and seeing her family settled.

Similarly, Rumi was also trying to find a suitable career for herself. After trying to become a music engineer and later working with young girls in the community, she decided to train as a psychotherapist. When Rumi was a baby in Pakistan, everyone thought her a very wise child, not clever or smart, but a wise and deeply intelligent person. Therefore, to become a psychotherapist was just the right thing for her. Everyone could see that she was sensitive and had a great ability to be empathetic. Rumi remembered that her ancestors were Sufis and Pirs who listened to people and practiced natural healing but were not noticed very much by the public, so she was continuing her family tradition. She became a great psychotherapist, and Naz was very proud of her. It made Naz very happy, and she felt that all the emotional roller coasters were behind her.

However, just as she had started to think like this, her Titanic sank, and the survivors were very badly hurt. On 23 August 1992, Naz left Gilgit and returned to Rawalpindi to fly back to London on 30 August. Due to walking a lot in Gilgit, Naz's ankles had swollen up a lot. Her sister-in-law suggested that she should go to see a famous Hakim [Herbalist] in Rawalpindi, who was also a family friend. Otherwise, the ankles would give her a lot of trouble because of the long flight to London. On the 26th of August, Naz and her sister-in-law went to see the Hakim, and this moment pinpointed one of the most tragic events of Naz's life. When they got back from the Hakim, Naz's mother told her that Rumi had rung and had said that she would call again later.

Around 8pm Pakistan time and 4pm London time, Omer's childhood friend George, who is still one of the family, rang and told Naz to sit down because he had bad news for her. Naz immediately thought about Rumi, but George told her that Omer was dead. He had died the night before at 10 o'clock and his body was in the Lighthouse hospice in Notting Hill. Naz could not see for a few minutes. It was dark in front of her eyes and her head felt like she had been hit by a truck. She could not take in this information, and she felt dizzy. Her sister brought some water for her to drink. Her mother was beating her breast and crying out loud and kept repeating that he was only 26 years old. Naz, her brothers, sister, and all the clan got together within an hour. Naz sat on the floor crossed legged, her eyes wide open all night and never said anything. Her brain was still trying to process the information, but everything was numb. She could hear people talking, but she did not know who they were or what they were saying.

Her father's tears fell nonstop, and he kept repeating that he didn't know who he was crying for most, whether it was for Naz or for Omer. He kept repeating, "my daughter worked so hard to bring her children up on her own and we thought her bad days were over." Naz was numb for days. She could not speak or eat or cry. Her father said to her, "Why are you not crying? Why have you become like stone?" He reminded her that when her uncle had died aged 22, she had cried so hard and asked what had happened to her. Now, why was she not crying? Naz's sister was hugging her and saying you must cry, otherwise you will be very ill. In Punjabi, it meant she would develop a serious ailment. Her childhood friends were trying to give her some food, but Naz was unable to eat. One of Naz's brothers said that overnight, his sister had aged twenty years.

On the 30th August, Naz left for London and her brother went with her to accompany her and help her. All the way to London, a seven-hour flight, Naz was still very quiet, looking out of the window and thinking, "Omer must be flying in these clouds."

Chapter 15

Türkiye

Naz became very depressed. She would cry for many hours on her own and when she got tired, she would become quiet for some time. But she got on with life, working and seeing some friends and family. Omer's friends, especially Lila and George, visited her often.

She abandoned the idea of the PhD as she no longer wanted to work on it and wanted to spend more time with her children, friends, and family. Her priorities changed; she felt she had missed a lot of time with the people she loved while she had been away. In the autumn of 2005, following her retirement, she decided to move back to Newcastle and spend as much time as she could with her two children.

At Easter 2005, one of Naz's friends invited her to spend a week at her holiday home on the Bodrum Peninsula in Türkiye. It was the first time that Naz had been to Bodrum and as soon as she landed in there, she fell in love with it; the hot weather at Easter, the blue skies, the stunning turquoise sea, the majestic mountains, and the flowers and fruits were all very familiar. It reminded Naz of Pakistan. Her favourite places in Bodrum were the high mountains and the markets where an abundance of fruits and vegetables were openly displayed, and people were not just buying a kilo or two kilos of tomatoes, but five or ten kilos. Naz loved the culture of buying food, cooking and eating together. She thought the atmosphere would help the healing process; years of hard work and pain would be washed away in the Aegean Sea.

Within a day or so of being in her friend's house, Naz decided to buy a house there. She was not going to rent or live in a hotel or wait and 'see what happens'. She was fully committed to buying her own home and living in Bodrum. She decided not to buy a place near her friend although though the house was close to a jetty and the very beautiful sea. The house was in a gated community where the houses were usually second homes – mostly for people from other cities in Türkiye like Istanbul or Ankara, but also for the Turkish diaspora who lived in places as far-flung as Australia and America.

It was a very well organised estate with beautiful houses and gardens. The roads were laid out beautifully, with plenty of greenery and white and pink oleanders spread out for miles. In the middle of the estate there was a shop and a restaurant with a wraparound terrace, and clear views of the sea for miles. The restaurant had an open wood-fired pizza oven, and the food was freshly cooked. At the back of the restaurant was a shop which was known as a market and all essentials were sold there. Outside the main gate was a main road where minibuses frequently ran to the local towns, Bodrum to the left and Turgutreis to the right.

Naz went to see some houses with the local estate agent and decided to buy a house in Turgutreis. This was a small town with one bank, one supermarket and a weekly big open market which sold everything you might need – fruit, vegetables, spices, plants, flowers, clothes, household goods. People would come from afar and spend the day in this small town. There were bars and restaurants where locals would go and then there were bars and restaurants on the sea front where the tourists would go to eat and drink. It was mostly local people who lived in this small town.

On the edge of the town, at the top of a steep hill going up a mountain, there was a beautiful village called Karabag, where the houses seemed to be just clinging to the side of the mountain. In between these white houses, there were different shades of bougainvillea, grapes, olive trees, apricots and several other fruits and flowers, making the village very picturesque. In the middle of the village, there was a beautiful mosque covered with grape vines and bougainvillea and its minarets stuck out. The only time people went into the mosque was for the Friday prayers or if there was a funeral. If someone passed away in the village, there would be an announcement in the mosque and people would get together for the funeral prayers. It is a tradition and part of the Muslim religion to join in with the funeral prayers and to walk with the funeral procession, even if the deceased is not known to you, until the deceased is taken into the nearby cemetery.

The local cemetery was on the best land in the area,

open with clear sea views and very beautiful and green with lovely trees for shade. It was close to the road and every time anyone passed through or by it, they would say a prayer for the deceased. Later, when Naz lived there, she wanted to be buried in this cemetery. She loved the fact that people from the community were coming and going, walking among the dead, and liked the idea of the living and the dead being side by side.

Next to this steep hill was another steep hill where houses were being built. The agent took Naz to see one of the houses, which had three bedrooms, two bathrooms, a living room and a kitchen. It was a big house with large rooms and balconies in the front, all with full sea views, looking towards the village mosque and some of the Greek islands. At the back was a thick forest with all sorts of wildlife. The roof had solar panels to heat the water in the winter.

When Naz entered the house, she saw the open turquoise sea and could see the Greek island, Kos, from her balcony. Although she was in Türkiye, her mobile was telling her that she was in Greece. The house was that close to Greece and Europe. She liked the house and after fifteen minutes she said yes to the agent and paid the deposit there and then. Naz knew that she was taking early retirement at the end of the summer term and that she would be able to pay for the house. So Naz bought a house in Karabag. Kara means black and Bag means garden. It was a garden with black olives, black grapes, and black mulberries everywhere. Naz thought the love of high mountains was in her genes as her ancestors came from a small village, Keruli, in a mountainous region, so she felt that she had come from the mountains of Keruli, now to the mountains around Karabag.

When Naz went back to her friend's house and told her that she had bought a house, her friend could not believe that Naz had bought a house within a few hours.

The houses are built for the summer in that area and in the winter, it rains a lot, so there are no proper provisions for heating. Naz decided to live there from Easter until autumn and to move back to Newcastle to spend winter and Christmas with the children.

Naz took early retirement that summer and went back to Karabag with her son Raza and his partner Romana in July. It was very hot, so they completed the paperwork and came back to England. While Naz was in Karabag, she was told that she could buy a complete package of household items in a package – everything she needed for a three-bedroomed house. It included a three-piece sofa, a set of tablecloths, a fridge and cooker, tea towels, bath towels, dining table and even air conditioning - everything one needs to live. So, she bought the package.

Naz went back in the autumn to move into the house. A big truck arrived with four local men who unloaded the truck, put everything in its place, and within a few hours, they left Naz with a fully furnished and clean home. Naz wanted a big marble dining table for the terrace because everyone would spend time around the table, and it would stay there through every season. One day, Naz spotted some people making furniture on the roadside. As the season was ending, the furniture makers were finishing off the orders before the rainy season started. Naz saw one furniture maker who was sitting at a distance from all others and seemed to have no work. When she went up close to him, Naz could see he had been drinking but was not drunk. Her social worker instinct came out, and she sat beside him and explained to him about her idea of a marble table on a sturdy wooden frame. The man understood what was required and asked for the deposit to buy a tree. After some deliberation, Naz handed over the deposit and the drawing and measurements of the dining table. Five days later, Naz went to see the progress. Yes, there was a tree there alright, but the man was lying beside the tree and he was very drunk. Naz had to leave for Newcastle a few days later, so she left the money and instructions with a neighbour to follow up with the table. When she came back in the spring, there was a beautiful marble table on her terrace.

Naz went to Bodrum city and bought lots of Ottoman prints, framed them nicely and hung them everywhere around the house. One of her favourite prints was 'the carpet seller.' There was a story that, in Ottoman times, there was a carpet seller on a street where men would come and pretend they were choosing carpets. On the other side of the street, there was a balcony with women in purdah wearing the veil standing behind a curtain. They were choosing a prospective husband. The carpet seller was not only aware of these dynamics, he was also part of it.

After hanging these prints, it felt like magic. Sunshine at the beginning of spring with the solar panels heating the water and an abundance of local fruits and vegetables. In the centre of Turgatries, there were local council offices surrounded by beautiful gardens and trees, and next to the offices was a children's playground with swings and slides. Naz would go to the offices to pay bills such as water, electricity or her taxes, and the officers were always very helpful and welcoming. She was reminded of Gilgit, where a lot of work was done with ease in a friendly atmosphere. The officers took extra care of the foreigners. The Council also operated a regular minibus service with minimum charges. It went up and down the hill from her house on a regular basis, from very early in the morning to very late at night. It was mostly used by locals and school children. On market days, the bus would be full of people, young children screaming, old people sweating in the heat, drunks looking very content, and some foreigners, usually British, as well as lots of fruits and vegetables.

Often the British preferred to walk up and down the hill with their shirts off even in the summer sun. Perhaps some were too drunk to notice the heat until it was too late and they were burned. There was a taxi stand near the council offices and a café where lots of taxis waited to take people to various locations; they made good money or market days.

There was just one local shop halfway down the hill, run by a woman called Gull Fida, meaning something like Rosy or Rose in English. She was in her late forties, a beautiful and strong looking woman. She also had some houses in the village which she would let out to the seasonal workers. She lived close to her shop in a nice big house with large gardens, full of all sorts of fruit and vegetables. Although the fruit and vegetables were very cheap in the market, all the locals grew vegetables and at least a lemon tree, no matter how little land they had. Gull Fida also had several cows which would walk up the hill on their own into the woods behind Naz's house and stay there until sunset and then go back home down the hill. This reminded Naz of her grandparents' village, Keruli, where all the goats from the village would go up the hill every morning and come back to the village in the evening. As a child, Naz could not understand how all the goats from the village got together in the morning and walked up to the pasture as one group and in the evening came down as one group. When they entered the village in the evening, they split up and went to their own homes without any help from people. Gull Fida's cows also came and went on their own. The cows and Gull Fida would help themselves to a drink from Naz's garden tap, whether Naz was around or not. Naz would always find out when she had to pay her water bill. She was familiar with this culture where informally neighbours have certain rights and take the liberty of doing this. Naz was aware that it was all give and take and one does not keep count. A few years later, when Naz's niece came to visit for a few months with three boys aged 12, 10 and 7 and a husband, Gull Fida not only let the boys feed the cows and direct them up the hill in the morning and down the hill in the evening but also showed them how to milk the cows. She also supplied them with free milk for their entire stay in Karabag. Those boys have grown up now and they still tell everyone their stories about Gull Fida and her generosity. Everyone in the Village knew and respected Gull Fida and no one would dare cross her path. Naz had seen Gull Fida arguing with the most powerful men in the village and she always stood her ground.

One of the first things Naz did was to visit all the nearby garden centres. To her delight, all the exotic flowers and vegetables which she had not been able to grow in England, she could now grow in Karabag and the plants were cheap to buy. Naz planted Melissa, Arabian jasmine, bougainvillea, oleander, lemons, oranges, pomegranates, aubergine and okra. She loved to watch the flowers growing so fast. The combination of good soil and sun made everything grow much brighter and sweeter and tastier.

By talking to the local women, Naz found out about the best beaches in the area. Naz had only learned to swim recently in a swimming pool. And prior to coming to Karabag, she had never swum in the sea. Although Newcastle and Northumberland had stunning beaches, it was too cold for Naz to swim in the sea, even in the summer. But the Aegean was very inviting, and she soon found out it was easier to swim in the sea than in a swimming pool.

Naz loved getting up early, particularly in the summer. Every morning, she would go for a swim just before sunrise. There would always be some local women on the beautiful, empty beach, including Gul Fida. There would be no one else around except these few women, no towels, no deck chairs, no lying on the beaches sunbathing. Just wild swimming. The sea at that time was so calm and blue and particularly clean at that time. They would all swim, chat, and laugh; the fresh air in the mornings and the sea breeze was something magical. Naz found that swimming was very relaxing and soothing. She would lie on her back in the sea, looking at the blue sky, comforted by the turquoise water and feel that she was embraced by love.

After swimming, Naz would go to her favourite bread shop and buy fresh bread. This bread shop was like no other and seemed like the favourite shop of lots of people. The bread was baked on the premises behind the counter in the shop, and you could see the dough going in and the most delicious bread coming out. It was baked on a wood fire and there were several different types of bread, including nans, pitas, biscuits, cakes and baklava. The men and women in the bread shop knew that Naz bought walnut bread so they would have it ready for her in the morning. She would pick up the bread and go back home, have a shower, and put on a long dress. She loved the fact that all she had to do was put on a dress, no shoes, at least at home. She always disliked wearing lots of clothes, and socks and shoes. Even in London in the winter, rather than wearing a jumper, she preferred a big Kashmiri shawl wrapped round her. She always enjoyed walking barefoot, and when she had lived in Glasgow, she would wear sandals until very late in the autumn. Now, she could enjoy the total freedom of not wearing too many clothes.

Naz would have a leisurely breakfast on the terrace at the marble table, with fresh bread, eggs and lots of coffee, looking at the Aegean and the island of Kos. There was no radio or television, but she had a regular delivery of the Weekly Guardian to the town post office. She had to go to the town to pick it up because the postman who was supposed to deliver the newspaper had told her his scooter was not strong enough to go up the hill so he couldn't deliver it. He told Naz that as she came into town every day, there was no reason why she couldn't pick it up herself. Naz thought it did make sense and there was no harm in picking up your own post. The postman was aware that Naz was in town almost every day. It was a small town and everyone knew almost everyone's business. Naz would also routinely go swimming in the evenings and watch the sunset. Then she would meet friends in town and have dinner with them, or eat in a restaurant by herself, or pick up some fish and come home for dinner.

Naz was aware that reputations mattered a lot in the small town and she was familiar with this type of community. It was similar in Pakistan and also in Gilgit. It has been said that in small places where everyone knows everyone, there is less chance of crime because it would be known and remembered for generations. Naz lived alone, which everyone was aware of, so she felt safe and lived there without any fear. In large towns where people are anonymous and transient, the possibilities of crime increase.

Part of the reason for living there was to catch up with all the things that Naz had not been able to do after recovering from an unhappy marriage, bringing up the family, training, and having very demanding jobs. She wanted to read all the books she had been wanting to read for years and wanted to spend more time quality time with her family. Since she had left Pakistan in 1963, she had been on such a roller coaster that she had never had time to recover. She had not even had time to grieve for her Uncle Tariq, who had died just a month before she left Rawalpindi. When she came to England, her husband not only prevented her from expressing her feelings, but she was also not allowed to share her feelings of grief in letters to her family in Rawalpindi. Naz had heard from many refugees that there was a difference in choosing to leave your country to being an exile. When you are sent away from your country, the recovery is difficult if not impossible. Naz felt that she was sent away to live with a stranger in a strange country without any family and friends for support.

She needed time to recover and wash away all the extra layers of painful experiences, and Karabag was the place where she felt she could do that. Some of Naz's liberal friends had suggested that she should be staying in England doing voluntary work in the community, rather than thinking of herself. But perhaps they did not understand that to recognise your own limits and ability to give is equally important. When you have given everything, and there is nothing left to give, it is counterproductive to carry on.

While living in Karabag, Naz had the opportunity to read all the books she could not read before, due to work. She would enjoy long uninterrupted periods of time – no traffic sounds, just the birds singing – where she could get lost in a book and enjoy every bit of it. Usually, after breakfast, she would sit on the terrace and read books written by people from different countries. Naz enjoyed the visits of her friends and family from all over the world – from Australia, South Africa, India, Canada and, of course, from Britain and Pakistan, her two homes. Some family and friends came over every year, some came a few times and others just once.

Lila, the family friend introduced by Omer many years

ago, was now living in London and came over every year for a couple of weeks. Naz and Lila would go swimming together, shop and cook. They would talk for hours and sometimes just enjoy each other's company. Lila called this their special time. The flights from London usually came overnight and landed very early in the morning. Once, Lila came over and got the bus from Bodrum Airport, which dropped her off in front of Naz's home. Still half asleep, Lila saw an open door and went inside and sat on the sofa. She did not realise that she was in the wrong house. The house belonged to a local family who were all getting on with their morning chores and they gave Lila a cup of tea. She sat there thinking that Naz had changed everything in the house and Naz must be having some visitors. The owner of the house was wondering why this English woman was sitting in their house, but didn't ask Lila why. After Lila had tea and had woken up a bit, she inquired about Naz and found out that she had been sitting in the wrong house all this time. Usually in the morning, Naz would leave her front door open in case she was in the shower and miss a visitor. Naz was waiting to have breakfast with Lila in her house, wondering where she had gone.

It was easy for Naz's family to visit her in Türkiye from Pakistan because the visas weren't a problem. In Britain, it's almost impossible to get a visa to visit unless you have lots of money and you are not from a developing country. So, Naz's family often had big reunions in Bodrum. One summer, Naz's two brothers and two nephews came from Pakistan, one brother came from America, and one brother and one nephew came from Canada. The last time they had all got together like that had been when they were children all living together in Rawalpindi. Everyone was very happy to be together, and they soon got into an easy routine. Naz would go swimming as usual. Some brothers and nephews would go with her, and others would stay at home to get the breakfast ready and clean the house.

One morning, Naz was having a shower and getting ready upstairs to join her brothers for breakfast when she heard her brothers talking in English. Naz could not understand why they were conversing in English, but when she came downstairs, she saw that one of her English friends, Joan, had arrived from London. She was sitting at the breakfast table having breakfast with Naz's brothers. They hadn't bothered to ask her who she was. They just assumed she must be their sister's friend and offered her breakfast.

Naz loved that sort of culture and atmosphere of open door where people can walk in and join a meal. Naz always cooked a lot, so it didn't matter if there were one or two people extra. Naz would cook pilau biryani, lamb curry, lots of salad and they would all sit and eat together like they used to when they were children in Rawalpindi. In Rawalpindi, Naz and her sister used to serve food to all her brothers. Now in Karabag, they were all grown up and shared the responsibility. Naz's brother from Pakistan, Naeem, insisted on washing the dishes and cleaning the kitchen. The brother from America, Shaukat, kept the house clean. Brother Suliman was lazy and just sat there and cracked jokes.

The young nephews and the visitors would sleep in the bedrooms with Naz, and the brothers would sleep on the roof under the stars. It was a big flat roof with a tiled floor. One of the brothers would wash the roof in the evening and put the mattresses on the floor. They would smoke and talk loudly until late, which didn't bother anyone. They had soap and shampoo there, so in the mornings, they would hose each other and leave Naz and her guests to use the shower downstairs. Sometimes, they would hire cars and go and visit places, or go on a boat trip, but mostly they would just enjoy staying at home and catching up with each other.

Once, when an old university friend, Linda, was visiting Karabag, they decided to go to Kos for a day. Kos is a beautiful island with the same lovely Aegean food and restaurants and lots of greenery and trees giving cool shade. When Naz and Linda were having lunch in the main town square, one of them suggested going to visit Colin and Trevor, who lived on another Greek island. This was the same Trevor who had been Naz's tutor more than twenty years before at Bradford University. Linda and Naz had got to know Colin and his partner Trevor, who was an external examiner, when Linda was at Manchester University and Naz was at Brunel University.

Neither Naz nor Linda knew where in Greece Colin and Trevor lived or even if they were in Greece at that moment. All they knew was that they lived on an island whose name began with S. They looked at the map and the name Samos sounded familiar. They went to the travel agent and bought two tickets to Samos, which was several islands further away from Kos. When they reached the harbour to board, they saw something like a huge straight black bicycle tube floating horizontally in the harbour. The door of the tube opened and the passengers in the queue started to get into it. Linda and Naz followed the other passengers and sat in their seats. This tube was like a hovercraft but was not a hovercraft and was nothing like they had ever seen before. The seats were quite uncomfortable, the windows were very small, and it felt like being stuck in a bicycle tube. It stopped at every little seaport on the islands. Some names were familiar, but others they had never heard of. Lots of young people, mostly 'hippy' types, got on and off, clearly on holiday or touring the islands. There were also lots of local people who had been to the markets or shopping or visiting families. There wasn't another couple like Naz and Linda, middle-aged and looking lost, not knowing where they were going.

After a good four hours, they arrived at Samos port. Taxis were waiting at the harbour for the passengers getting off the ferries. Naz asked a taxi driver to take them to Samos and negotiated a price. The village of Samos spreads out on the slopes around the port and after a few miles, the Taxi driver dropped them at the bottom of the village, which was also the bottom of a mountain. They walked for a while until they came across a young man and asked him where Colin and Trevor lived in the village. He said he didn't know them but that he knew someone who would know. The young man walked with Linda and Naz and took them to a shop where a woman of similar age to Linda and Naz was serving the customers. The young man asked her something in Greek and she said yes. After serving the customers, she closed the shop and asked Linda and Naz to follow her up the mountain.

This shop keeper walked much faster than Linda and Naz, climbing the mountain like a goat whereas Linda and Naz were huffing and puffing, and trailing behind. There were narrow cobbled streets which were very clean and beautiful, and old houses with geraniums, bougainvillea and other local flowers clinging to their walls. All the doors and shutters were painted in Aegean blue colours and most of the front doors were open. Naz thought this was a very positive sign of a good, friendly village.

By the time they reached the top of the hill, about thirty other people from the village had joined them on their walk. At the top, the place looked like a scene from an art film. You could see the entire Mediterranean Sea where the Aegean meets the Mediterranean. There were stunning flowers and gardens with olives, apricots, plums and pomegranate flowers, as well as mimosa trees. The house they were aiming for was on an open terrace so that you could step on to the terrace from the street; there was no gate so you couldn't tell where the street ended, and the private terrace started. The house was attached to one side of the terrace and the house was on several levels - the kitchen and a living room ran straight from the terrace, the bedrooms were downstairs, and then there was a basement attached to the kitchen garden.

When they all walked onto the terrace, there was Colin, sitting on a chair facing the Mediterranean, his back to the entrance and reading *The Kite Runner*. When he heard people talking, he turned round and could not understand what was going on. He looked very confused and didn't recognise Naz and Linda because it had been a very long time since he had

215

seen them and also Naz's skin was much darker, due to living in Türkiye. To see the two women out of place was totally unexpected. Trevor was in the kitchen cooking the evening meal and when he came out, likewise, it took him a while to adjust to the situation.

The local people who accompanied the visitors were waiting in the courtyard, looking for an explanation. Colin could see that the crowd would not leave until he explained the visitors' relationship with the two hosts. Trevor introduced Naz and Linda, their friends and former colleagues. The people asked where they had come from and Colin replied that they had come from England and were British. People from the village said that yes, Linda was British, but the darker woman could not be British. Naz was thinking, "Here we go again - perhaps the news that dark people have landed on the shores of England has not reached this village of Samos." Then Linda said that actually Naz was British, and she herself was not British but Irish. The crowd left, shaking their heads in utter disbelief.

Trevor brought the dinner out on the terrace and they all exchanged their news and had a really good conversation. Trevor showed them the house and the kitchen garden, which was absolutely like something from the magazine *House and Garden*. As the house was clinging to the mountain, it was naturally built vertically. One of the lowest level rooms, which was adjacent to the kitchen garden, was full of preserved fruit and vegetables, olives, and olive oil. Trevor and Colin had land on the mountain where they grew all the fruit and vegetables as well as their olives. They had got together with some people in the village and bought an olive pressing machine, so they had their own oil vial. Naz thought it was typical of Trevor to be so meticulous and well organised.

Next morning, Trevor brought coffee in bed for Naz and sat beside her and asked her about her family and the present situation. All the time, Naz was thinking that she had been so lucky to have Trevor, who was so sensitive and gentle, as her tutor. He had been so respectful of women who went to university later in life and he made sure that women like Naz had all the opportunities available. After breakfast, Linda and Naz said their goodbyes and started on their journey back to Karabag.

Ten years after buying the house, Naz became ill and could no longer live in Türkiye on her own. So, she sold the house to the first person who came to buy it because she knew her children were not interested in keeping it. As she was having chemotherapy, she could not take anything from the house except her books, which she gave to the local book seller. Some people thought she had thrown away the house and everything in it but her son Raza, who could always say something clever on these occasions said, "Mum, just think of all the very good times you had there with your friends and family, they are priceless." Naz agreed, especially as some of the people with whom she had spent those happy times were not around anymore.

Chapter 16

Naseeb

Naz is in her garden in London feeding the birds and thinking that she is lucky to have some very unusual birds visiting from the nearby Wetlands Centre and the parakeets from the nearby trees. There are also local birds like bluetits, robins and magpies which remind her of Newcastle. Facing the end of her life, she has started to think about the beginning of her life, having been born in North India and moving to what became Pakistan. At that time, her parents' house was full of people, having three generations in one house, uncles, aunties, and grandparents. However, now towards the end, in London, Naz is living on her own. The journey from her Pakistani lifestyle to a British lifestyle was not very easy much of the time. Naz's parents died more than twenty years ago, and some of her siblings have either passed away or left Pakistan. Now hardly any close relatives live in Rawalpindi and Naz has minimum connections to the country where she lived until she was eighteen. Naz reflects on her life and how her elders dealt with the end of their lives with courage and without medical intervention. She is drawing strength from her memories of their realistic attitudes to life and death.

She remembered that her great grandfather, Mohammed Ali Shah, lived on his own in his village during the last days of his life because that was what he wanted to do. This was very unusual in those days, almost unheard of in the village. His sons, daughter, and grandchildren all lived very close to him and looked after him. They cooked and cleaned and did everything for him. Stubbornness and determination ran in the family, and he would not let anyone live with him, whatever anyone said. Moreover, if it had been up to him, he would have laid on the top of the highest mountain and waited for the Azrael, the angel of death, like native Indian Americans. Mohammed Ali Shah lived on a mountain and did die there, albeit indoors. The family was concerned that their old man was sleeping on his own. They wanted to be with him, but also felt that allowing him to be alone would give the family a bad name. But Muhammed Ali Shah would not have it any other way. The night that he was dying, his children begged him to let them stay with him, but he didn't listen to them. However, he promised them that he would leave the door open so that when he was dead, they didn't have to break the door down to get in.

The next morning just before dawn, when his daughters and grandchildren arrived as usual, the door was open and Muhammed Ali Shah had died. His body was still warm, and the chain on the door was still moving, as if Azrael had just left and had taken his soul away.

Later, the men of the family came and gave Muhammed Ali Shah his last bath, according to his wishes. He wanted Imperial Leather soap to be used for his last wash, and he had purchased this especially for the occasion some months earlier. After the bath, he was wrapped in a white cotton cloth and his body was brought out into the courtyard for people to view. By that time, the entire village had arrived, as well as relatives from other villages and the cities.

Muhammed Ali Shah used to feed the birds every morning and on the morning of his death, all the birds arrived as usual. One of his daughters remembered that he fed the birds, so she put the food out for them. But all the birds just sat on the wall whilst Muhammed Ali Shah's body was being prepared and didn't eat the food. Then, they left when the body was taken away for the burial. The birds never came back to the house again. Similarly, at dawn, it was usual for Muhammed Ali Shah's goats to go up the mountains to the higher pastures by themselves, but on that day they didn't. They just hung around all day and watched his body being taken away for the funeral. Naz's great grandfather was the last member of the family to die in the mountains. He had had a tough life, as mountain people had, but he came from courageous people who believed in the afterlife and he died peacefully having lived a full life.

Naz also loves to feed the birds in the morning. A love of nature and animals is something that was passed down from her ancestors, as well as other rituals and practices. She believes that people often adopt certain family practices and rituals unconsciously. She reflects that often, people continue these traditions without really understanding the reason why the elders practiced them and without understanding how they viewed life. Now, at the end of her life, Naz has started to reflect on these things, particularly the way her elders faced death with confidence and courage. The belief is that death is part of life, and they feel lucky, satisfied and contented that they have lived until old age. Naz takes courage herself from this heritage, despite the fact that her life took her in a very different direction.

Naz also thinks about her grandfather Haider Shah, who died in Rawalpindi. During the last days of his life, he had his bed close to the window, which was kept open in winter as well as summer. When Naz heard that her grandfather was ill and possibly dying, she went to Rawalpindi to see him and the entire biradari was in his house. Haider Shah was sitting up on his bed and looking out of the window. When he saw Naz, he was very happy and told her that he had been waiting for her. He said that he had been fighting and arguing with Azrael about who he wanted to come before he died and said his first-born grandchild Naz had to come. Once Naz was there, he told her, Azrael could come anytime and do his job. Haider Shah and Naz talked all night. Naz told him that she remembered him as a young man because she was the oldest grandchild. She mentioned a story told to her by her grandmother, of when he retired at still a relatively young age, and left his job to go back and live in his home village of Kuroli. It was a story that was told over and over again. It was about his twin sister's rivalry and her revenge, which amused the family for generations. Naz's grandfather was surprised that she still remembered that, and they both had a good laugh. She also reminded him about how he taught her to cook, which has been a skill she has used all through her life. After a few days, Naz said goodbye to her grandfather and left for England. Haider Shah died soon after that. Naz remembered the warmth and love from her grandfather. She felt by living in Britain for most of their childhoods, her children had missed the experience of grandparents' love and closeness.

At a death, people in Pakistan cry out loud, scream, wail, and beat their breast, both men and women. When they get tired, they talk and eat together. According to the Muslim religion, the deceased are buried as soon as possible. Recently, this practice has become slightly different, especially in Britain. The deceased are not always buried immediately, sometimes due to administrative reasons. Sometimes, people prefer their bodies to be taken to their former countries and buried there, but nowadays, most people are buried in Britain. Possibly one reason is that the elders have passed away in Pakistan but also, as most of the people lived their lives in this country, there is no reason for them to be buried in Pakistan.

The common belief is that the deceased's spirit is not settled for forty days and keeps coming back to the person's house, so the extended family members stay in the home for forty days. Family members take turns to buy and cook food for everyone, including the visitors who come to give their condolences. Socially, it is a good practice because the family cry together, talk about the deceased, and tell stories about the person. Religious people read the Quran and other religious books or religious stories. That is how the grief and the tension are released.

When Naz was in Rawalpindi and heard that her son Omer had died, she kept saying that she had not seen him for months and was looking for him everywhere but could not see him. Naz's father, who was also crying out loud, sat beside Naz and told her a story which is in the Quran as well as the Bible, and possibly in the Tora too about prophets. The story is about Joseph, who disappeared for months. His father, Jacob, who loved his son very much, looked for him everywhere. When he could not find him, Jacob cried so much that he lost his eyesight. The purpose of telling this story was that death and loss happen to everyone, even to those who were prophets and the messengers of God. People tell stories like this to make the closest relative feel better.

Things have changed now, even in Pakistan, but when the extended family lived together, children were very close to adults. There was usually more than one woman in the household who was called mother, and there were different terms for mother, as well as for grandmother, father and grandfather, especially in Punjabi and Urdu, which are interchangeable. For example, Haider Shah's wife was Naz's grandmother, as was his sister, Taj Bi Bi. In extended families, children were brought up by all the adult relatives. When Naz first came to Britain and told people that she had several grandmothers, no one understood. When 'grandmothers' or 'uncles' died in Pakistan and people in Britain wanted to go on compassionate leave to Pakistan, these relatives were not considered by employers to be close enough.

Naz often thinks back to the time when she bought the house that she currently lives in. When she first moved in, it was full of all sorts of things, like old foreign currency, medals, and cheap knickknacks from all over the world. The previous owners' entire lives were laid out in this house. A couple had lived there, and the clothes of a very old lady hung in the bedroom, and shoes still lay on the floor. In the cellar which was initially built for coal storage, there were still pieces of coal lying around, and in the narrowest part of the room there was a bed with some old rags, like bedclothes. After some investigation, Naz found out that the previous owner was a soldier who had obviously travelled around the world and collected the knickknacks. The woman had died first, and it seemed that the old man had spent his last years sleeping in a dark and airless cellar – perhaps as a reminder of how he slept in the trenches during the war. It is likely that he had been mentally unwell.

When Naz saw all this, she asked the estate agent to ask the relatives who were inheriting the estate if they would like to take anything from the house, for example, photographs, medals or anything else. Naz was very sad to find out that no one in the family was interested in anything and they were happy for Naz to dispose of everything. This had an impact on her in a very strange way. It made her think that people go around the world collecting bits and pieces and take pleasure in them, but in the end, they often don't mean anything to others unless they have monetary value. Life goes on and people have their own interests and their own material objects that are important to them. Naz had often felt that her children were not interested in her Pakistani heritage, but she knows that she nevertheless passed on some of her skills and values. The memories of the life journey that they shared will continued, along with the love and warmth that they share.

Naz thinks about where her life had started in Britain and where it is going to end. Prior to her marriage with Yunis and coming to Britain, Naz had never thought about marriage. She had thought she would complete her education in Pakistan and be a sporty type of person like her father and jump from parachutes as he did. If a marriage had been arranged for her, she had imagined it would be someone from the Airforce. Her husband would be tall, handsome, broad minded and a very kind man like her father or Uncle Tariq. After her Nikah with Yunis, she thought she would complete her education in Britain and have a nice home with gardens where she could grow flowers and vegetables like her mother. But it turned out to be the opposite of this with Yunis.

When she came to Britain, she was eighteen years old and a very young eighteen. She had been bitterly disappointed, not so much about the poverty but about the lies and deception that had taken place. She very quickly learned to be patient. For many years, she thought she had no option but to stay in the marriage until things got better. No one ever divorced in the biradari and what could she do anyway, without any qualifications and with three children? She did not want to hurt her parents by telling them the truth and leaving her husband. She could not see an end to the poverty and the cruelty and, unfortunately, things did not get any better as the marriage proceeded. Now, she wonders where she got the strength from to fight and struggle for so many years.

She remembers once in 1973, when the family was living in a damp and cold council flat, she was sitting in a park in Gateshead with her three children and telling them that everything would be good, that they would have money, nice food and a nice home. She believed in that. Now she wonders how she could have believed it was possible in those circumstances.

Looking back, Naz thinks that if she had spent her married life in Pakistan, with her family around, perhaps Yunis would not have been so cruel. Things might have been better. Yunis might have been more relaxed and aware of the reactions of the extended family to his behaviour. On the other hand, it is also possible there would have been more pressure on Naz to stay with Yunis, for the sake of the family honour.

So, on reflection, Naz thinks that it was better that she had been in Britain and did not have any family pressure to either put up with Yunis, or to remarry. There was no family support, but this also meant that she was free to make her own decisions and chose her own path. In England, there were also well-established institutions like Social Services and the Education Department to support her. Britain's welfare services are some of the best in the world, or at least they were then, especially for women on their own who wished to rebuild their lives. Now, the only family that Naz has in Britain are her son Raza and daughter Rumi, and they both live in different parts of the country – in the North of England. But Naz has friends in London, including a very old and close friend Lila, who she knows will be with her when the time comes.

Both Naz's children have worked as therapists. Naz thinks about how all three of her children inherited this caring approach from their ancestors and are naturally compassionate, kind, and empathic. The elders, men and women, in Naz's family were spiritual healers and people came to them to share their problems. The elders would listen to them and advise them and help them if they could. Even now, some members of the extended family do spiritual healings and people visit them for that purpose. In the 1960s, lots of hippies from the West went to Rawalpindi and when they ran out of money or fell ill, Naz's family would bring them home and look after them, giving them ginger tea and other herbs as well as spiritual healing.

Naz has discussed her end-of-life plan with her children. She would like to die on her big sofa where she spends lots of time nowadays. She can see her garden from the sofa, the changing sky and weather, and the changing seasons. Rumi told her not to worry, that she will put her bed next to the sofa and be holding Naz's hand, and Raza has reassured her that he will have her head on his lap.

Naz knows that her children have been her greatest strength and support throughout. She had them at such a young age that they almost grew up with her. They have been part of all the ups and downs and are able to communicate openly and discuss every issue. They have chosen their own paths in life. Naz's own path has especially been about promoting equality, not just gender equality, but also equality of wealth and between the races. She feels that women of her generation made a major contribution in pushing forward the agenda of gender and race equality in particular.

When Naz was named Naseeb by the family, it was because her parents had their first child at such a young age and it was a girl, and because she was darker than her parents – signs to fear for her 'naseeb' in her culture. In Naz's case, it was the entire family's naseeb that the first child was a girl. When a daughter is born first in the family, especially in those days, everyone fears that there will be many difficulties to face, particularly when the parents are so young. The name Naseeb was given to Naz because it was her grandparents' wishes and her parents went along with it. They partly believed in destiny, though their beliefs changed as they grew older.

They say at the end of life that people start to remember back to the beginning of their life and start to reminisce. Naz now realises that when she was younger and studying or working, she was always forging ahead and did not have time to look back. She even started to forget some of the words in her original languages as well as certain aspect of her culture. But now, with social media and several Pakistani television channels available, it is all coming back to her.

Perhaps it was in Naz's naseeb to go to an English school in Pakistan and then come to Britain and struggle for survival for many years. For Naz, it was a good naseeb, because she learned so much. She was exposed to all sorts of situations, good and bad. She learned to fight for what she believed in and when she lost, she always remained optimistic, thinking things would change for the better and when she won, she would stay humble. This she learned from Mumtaz and Shahjahan particularly. Shahjahan was a sports man and used to take Naseeb and Farah to hockey matches. He always said that losing is part of life, and not to be too disheartened when you lose, and be humble when you win.

Some English friends who have visited and stayed with Naz's parents in Rawalpindi often comment about Naz's current situation, like living alone at this stage of her life. They have seen in Rawalpindi how young family members look after the elders, from cutting their toenails to feeding them by hand. The elders just pray all the time and prepare themselves to meet their maker. Her friends think Naz has lost out on this opportunity. She looked after the elders when she was young, but now that she is old, she does not have the extended family around to look after her.

Naz is now the oldest member of the clan. If she was in Rawalpindi now, she would be sitting on the charpai (bed) with a white dopata (scarf) covering her head and the prayer beads in her hand. She would still be making decisions in the extended family and involved in their life and death decisions. As an elder in the family, she would be making sure that the family traditions were adhered to and continue.

Instead, in London, it is the opposite. She does not have to make any decisions regarding the family. She leaves her bedroom in the morning and does not go back until the end of the day. In London nowadays, there is often little difference between younger people's clothes and older people's clothes, and Naz wears any clothes she likes. There are no constraints, no value judgements.

She thinks about her death and her two children, who she will be leaving behind with no family in Britain. But she knows that they are capable, independent, and caring people who will manage their lives well.

Thinking about the name Naseeb meaning destiny, she had never really believed in such a thing. She always believed that things would get better, that they couldn't remain the same. She knew that she had to fight, and she believed that this and the inner strength she had from her upbringing would see her through. She didn't believe in 'destiny' or fate and feels she has carved her own way in life.

However, although she doesn't believe in naseeb, looking back on her life, she can't help thinking about its meaning and reflecting on it. She thinks about the fantastic people she has met who contributed to her life and helped her to move forward in a positive way. Her parents were very strong people who gave her a good solid beginning in life as a child – love, warmth and a free-thinking mind. Could this be what influenced her 'naseeb'? Could it be this that especially helped her develop a free-thinking mind?

Naz thinks about how her possible 'naseeb' could be judged. Was it a good naseeb or a bad one? The word 'naseeb' is used to define either outcome. For example, on the subcontinent, if you don't achieve or obtain something, you could say it was not in my naseeb. But if you do, you can also say it was in my naseeb. There are similar ideas in Britain, in sayings like 'it wasn't meant to be,' or 'my name was written on it.' Some people fully believe in destiny, many partly believe in it, and others not at all. Some use it a as 'throwaway' line, not meaning anything serious. Some change their beliefs through life. Naz feels her free-thinking mind was the basis for how her life evolved, but she wouldn't put this down to naseeb/destiny.

Naz helped her parents in later life, although they were reluctant initially to accept it. It was seen as embarrassing in Pakistani culture for men to accept help because they were meant to be the providers. She always remembered that at the end of her parents' lives, they said to Naz that she had been very good to them and had been like a son. This sentence stayed with Naz forever after. Naz said to them that she was a strong, independent, free minded, successful woman. Paradoxically, her life became very different from what was suggested by the name given to her at birth as a female first-born child, Naseeb.